# 7 TWELVE

# 7TWELVE

## A Diversified Investment Portfolio with a Plan

# CRAIG L. ISRAELSEN

WILEY

John Wiley & Sons, Inc.

Published by John Wiley & Sons, Inc., Hoboken, New Jersey.
Published simultaneously in Canada.

7Twelve™ is a trademark of Craig L. Israelsen

For general information on our other products and services or for technical support, please contact our Customer Care Department within the United States at (800) 762-2974, outside the United States at (317) 572-3993 or fax (317) 572-4002.

Wiley also publishes its books in a variety of electronic formats. Some content that appears in print may not be available in electronic books. For more information about Wiley products, visit our web site at www.wiley.com.

*Library of Congress Cataloging-in-Publication Data*

Israelsen, Craig L.
  7twelve : a diversified investment portfolio with a plan / Craig L. Israelsen.
     p.   cm.
  Includes index.
  ISBN 978-0-470-60527-1 (cloth); 978-0-470-64985-5 (ebk);
  978-0-470-64986-2 (ebk); 978-0-470-64987-9 (ebk)
  1. Portfolio management.   2. Investments.   I. Title.   II. Title: 7
twelve.   III. Title: Seven twelve.
  HG4529.5.I87 2010
  332.6—dc22                                                     2010004724

Printed in the United States of America

10 9 8 7 6 5 4 3 2 1

*Building rockets is complex. Building a diversified portfolio shouldn't be. This book isn't about rockets.*

# CONTENTS

Foreword                                                      xi

Preface                                                      xiii

Acknowledgments                                             xvii

Chapter 1   **A Recipe for Success**                           1
            The 7Twelve Recipe                                 2
            Salsa Anyone?                                       4
            U.S. Stock                                          7
            Non-U.S. Stock                                     12
            Real Estate                                        15
            Resources                                          16
            U.S. Bonds                                         19
            Non-U.S. Bonds                                     21
            Cash                                               22
            The Complete Recipe                                23

Chapter 2   **Lining Up the Ingredients**                     29
            A Recipe That Goes Waaay Back                      32
            Getting Better and Better                          34

Chapter 3   **The More Ingredients, the Better**              37
            Measuring Volatility and Risk                      38
            Diversification by Design                          40
            Diversification Requires Depth
            *and* Breadth                                      48

# Contents

Chapter 4    **Growth of Money**    **53**
Why Measure Growth of Money?    54
Expect Ups and Downs    56

Chapter 5    **Combining Ingredients That Zig *and* Zag**    **63**
Getting Close to Zero    64
Finding Assets That Play Nicely Together    65
Don't Forget Broad Diversification    68
Quantifying Correlation    73

Chapter 6    **Stirring the Mix**    **79**
Rebalancing versus Buy-and-Hold    80
Choosing a Schedule    86

Chapter 7    **Adjusting the Secret Sauce**    **89**
The Saving Years and the Spending Years    91
How Portfolio Mechanics Change in the Golden Years    94
Allocation Age versus Chronological Age    96
Life Stage Portfolios    98

Chapter 8    **How Long Will My Nest Egg Last?**    **105**
Survival of the Fittest    106
Reviewing the Nest Egg Guidelines    113

Chapter 9    **Should I Tilt toward Value or Growth?**    **117**
Does It Make a Difference?    118
The 7Twelve's Value Bias    125

Chapter 10    **Should I Jump in or Let the Pot Simmer?**    **129**
To Stir or Not to Stir?    130
The 7Twelve Works Both Ways    133
But If You *Still* Can't Decide . . .    135

# Contents

Chapter 11    **A Better 401(K)**    **137**
Switching the Default    137
Introducing Target Date
Funds and Balanced Funds    138
The 7Twelve Portfolio Approach    139
Determining Your Lifecycle Phase    144
Mismatch 101    147

Chapter 12    **The Problem of Undersaving**    **151**
Chasing Returns Is a Loser's Game    152
Add Plenty of Patience,
Perspective, and Persistence    156

Chapter 13    **Of Stocks, Bonds, and Risk**    **159**
A Tale of Two Time Frames    159
The "Diversification" Premium    166

Chapter 14    **Assembling Your Portfolio**    **171**

Chapter 15    **3 Secrets + 4 Principles =**
**7Twelve Perfection**    **181**

About the Author    187

Index    189

# FOREWORD

I first encountered Craig Israelsen's work on portfolio construction—that is, how to combine investments effectively and systematically so that your assets will grow over time—in 2005, when I became the editor in chief of *Financial Planning* magazine. At first, I found his efforts mystifying—he took a deep, deep dive into decades of performance data, sliced it up, and found patterns I had never encountered. Then, he described what he found in simple English—no flights of calculus or abstruse concepts to make him seem too smart to be questioned. At first, it seemed too simple to me to be as rigorous as it really is.

After a few months, I came to realize that Craig's ideas, like so many great thoughts, seem simple just because they are true. Like many deep insights, his are the kind that make you say to yourself, "Of course—why didn't I think of that before." And after years of intense conversations about the ins and outs of portfolio construction, and invigorating exchanges of research ideas, I am delighted to say that Craig is one of those rare souls who can create intellectual elegance out of chaotic and sometimes contradictory facts. This is what makes his work appear to be so simple, and what makes learning from him such a pleasure.

Which brings me to the subject of this book, *7Twelve,* a collection of investments that can dependably build wealth for an investor's entire life. I think of this portfolio as the culmination of Craig's research. He has taken the many varied techniques of portfolio construction and distilled them into a reasonable, workable system that any individual can execute, either on his or her own or with the help of a financial advisor. Once again, the ease of this system is deceptive, as it integrates the most contemporary research with Craig's own investigations to come up with his ultimate recipe for long-term success.

How does the 7Twelve portfolio work? It molds the confusing world of investments into a system that requires just a little regular upkeep. It is not greedy. It is a collection of mutual funds, index funds, or exchange-traded funds that covers a wide variety of assets, from stocks and bonds to real estate and commodities, so it should enable you to profit when certain assets grow and protect you from losing too much when certain types of assets drop in value.

During the past two years, after the financial markets' near collapse in 2008 and its rocket-powered recovery in 2009 and 2010 (at least so far), people have lost faith in the ability of markets to reflect the true value of things. Money that people saved for years, even decades, disappeared, and much of that vanished wealth never returned. It was a harsh lesson for those who staked their future on the stock market—which was most of us.

It is disappointing but not difficult to understand why real estate prices dropped, and why they have not returned. But why did stocks fall so precipitously, and then rise again so rapidly? Why did they drag down so many other assets, too? How can one protect savings from that kind of disaster without eliminating any possibility of long-term growth?

A widely diversified portfolio that is rebalanced systematically, like the 7Twelve, is a good start toward answering those questions. What's more, the 7Twelve method ratchets down your exposure to market risk as you age, thereby consolidating and protecting your long-term gains.

The 7Twelve method is not rapid-fire and is not designed to get you rich. It may not be exciting. But it is useful, and its clarity and simplicity belie its sophistication. Try it—you just may like it.

MARION ASNES

March 2010

# PREFACE

7Twelve™ provides a recipe for building a multi-asset investment portfolio with 12 low-cost mutual funds. The recipe is more important than the ingredients. A poor recipe with good ingredients produces a poor end product. A great recipe with average ingredients produces an acceptable outcome. A great *recipe* with great *ingredients* is the ideal scenario—and this book provides information about both.

Too many investors have portfolios that lack diversification breadth. A few mutual funds that seem different are often cobbled together. 7Twelve, on the other hand, is a diversified, multi-asset portfolio by design.

In addition to providing a recipe for a diversified portfolio, 7Twelve also provides guidance on portfolio management over the entire lifecycle. From our early working years to the years beyond retirement, the 7Twelve portfolio can be adapted to meet our ever-changing personal and family circumstances.

The 7Twelve plan is rich in supporting historical performance data. No conjecture here. No Ph.D. needed either. The information is presented simply so that a person who is relatively new to the field of investing can easily grasp and implement the 7Twelve portfolio recipe.

The 7Twelve will be of value to young investors as they start building their investment portfolios; to middle-aged individuals who need to start ratcheting down the risk of their portfolios as they move closer to retirement; and to retirees who need to ensure that their retirement portfolio is durable and insulated from large losses. Very simply, investors of any age can benefit from the guidance in 7Twelve. Everyone is welcome in this kitchen.

The book is organized into 15 bite-sized chapters. Chapters 1 and 2 introduce the 7Twelve recipe for building a diversified, multi-asset investment portfolio, and Chapter 3 demonstrates how our diversification is actually achieved. Many investors are less diversified than they think.

Chapter 4 introduces various ways to meaningfully measure portfolio performance. Chapter 5 outlines the performance benefits of building a low correlation portfolio. Chapters 6 and 7 focus on the ongoing management of the 7Twelve portfolio—from periodic rebalancing to changes in the asset allocation over the lifecycle.

From there, Chapter 8 addresses the poignant issue of portfolio durability during the retirement years. Chapters 9 and 10 present research results on two much debated investing topics: value versus growth and active versus passive. Chapter 11 sheds light on two very prominent types of mutual funds offered in 401(k) retirement plans: target date funds and balanced funds.

Dilemmas created by undersaving are covered in Chapter 12. And then Chapter 13 investigates the equity premium and how that issue has a huge effect on how investment portfolios are built. Chapter 14 is a summary, outlining mutual funds and exchange-traded funds that could be used as the ingredients in the 7Twelve recipe.

Chapter 15 is the simple, *simple* summary of a straightforward portfolio design.

For the reader who just can't get enough, my website (www.7TwelvePortfolio.com) contains monthly performance updates for the 7Twelve portfolio. In addition, there is downloadable software (an Excel spreadsheet) that allows you to compare the performance of other portfolios to the 7Twelve portfolio over various time periods that you control.

## Author's Disclaimer

Past performance of the 7Twelve portfolio is not a guarantee of future performance. This book does not represent investment advice nor is it an investment solicitation.

# ACKNOWLEDGMENTS

I appreciate the help of Meg Freeborn, Bill Falloon, Tiffany Charbonier, and Chris Gage of John Wiley & Sons in getting this book produced in a timely fashion.

My deepest appreciation will always be reserved for my eternal companion Tammy. I love her. And just as important, I trust and respect her. Our children are great, too, and I love them each in a very individual way: Sara and Jon, Andrew and Shannon, Heidi, Mark, Nathan, Emma, and Jared.

My parents, as well as Tammy's parents, have provided a lifelong example of integrity and endurance that has blessed our lives and the lives of our children.

Thanks also to Bob Vaughan, Robert Katz, Bryce Kurfees, and Andy Martin—each helpful in the early development of the 7Twelve portfolio.

Anciently, and almost cross-culturally, most numbers had an assigned symbolic meaning. So when people heard or read the number seven, for example, they were reminded of ideas of fullness and completion.

—Gaskill, Alonzo, *The Lost Language of Symbolism*

(Deseret Book)

# CHAPTER 1

# A RECIPE FOR SUCCESS

A wise chef follows a good recipe. Likewise, wise investors should have a good recipe they follow when building a portfolio. The 7Twelve Portfolio is that recipe. By following it, investors will build a diversified, multi-asset portfolio.

The 7Twelve portfolio invests in "7" core asset classes (or investment categories) by utilizing "Twelve" underlying mutual funds—hence the name 7Twelve. The 7Twelve portfolio has both depth and breadth. 7Twelve has diversification *depth* within each separate mutual fund, and diversification *breadth* across seven core asset classes.

## The 7Twelve Portfolio Recipe

| 7 Core Asset Classes | | | | | | |
|---|---|---|---|---|---|---|
| U.S. Stock | Non-U.S. Stock | Real Estate | Resources | U.S. Bonds | Non-U.S. Bonds | Cash |

| 12 Underlying Mutual Funds | | | | | | |
|---|---|---|---|---|---|---|
| Large Companies | Developed Companies | Real Estate | Natural Resources | Aggregate Bonds | International Bonds | U.S. Cash |
| Medium-sized Companies | Emerging Companies | | Commodities | Inflation-Protected Bonds | | |
| Small Companies | | | | | | |

7Twelve represents a complete portfolio by itself because it incorporates 12 different mutual funds. Alternatively, 7Twelve can be used as the starting point, or core component, in virtually any portfolio. The success of the 7Twelve portfolio is not the result of special skill. Rather, the success of the 7Twelve portfolio is the result of genuine diversification across multiple asset classes. The various mutual funds within the 7Twelve portfolio complement each other because they behave differently—the essential benefit of diversification.

Achieving diversification is critical to success in so many aspects of life. For example, only by combining a wide variety of very different instruments can an orchestra produce beautiful music. In the world of sports, the analogies abound. Teams combine players with different talents in order to maximize their chances for success.

Likewise, only by combining a wide variety of asset classes can an investment portfolio produce superior performance with lower levels of risk. Better risk-adjusted performance is the benefit from building broadly diversified investment portfolios.

## The 7Twelve Recipe

Think of the 7Twelve model as a recipe for building a broadly diversified investment portfolio with 12 different mutual funds—where each mutual fund is itself a diversified investment product.

For those new to investing, a mutual fund is a collection of stocks, bonds, or any other investable asset. Mutual funds are purchased in shares, just as stock in a company is purchased in units called shares. The difference being that mutual funds represent a diversified collection of "stuff," whereas a single issue of stock is not diversified. Building a portfolio using a wide variety of mutual funds is an ideal way to achieve maximum diversification. The trick is putting the right types of mutual funds together so that redundancy is avoided and diversification is maximized. Welcome to the 7Twelve portfolio "recipe"—your guide to building a portfolio that provides an ideal blend of risk-controlled performance.

As shown in Figure 1.1, each mutual fund has an equal share in the 7Twelve recipe, meaning that each mutual fund is equally valued for its specific contribution to the overall portfolio's performance.

## 7TWELVE

The 7Twelve is a diversified portfolio of 12 different mutual funds— where each mutual fund is itself a diversified investment product.

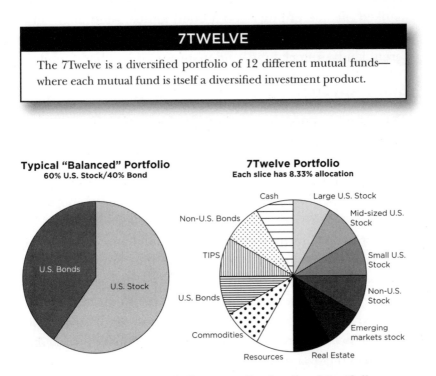

Typical "Balanced" Portfolio
60% U.S. Stock/40% Bond

7Twelve Portfolio
Each slice has 8.33% allocation

Figure 1.1 Two-Fund Portfolio versus Twelve-Fund Portfolio

The pie chart on the right (the multi-asset 7Twelve portfolio) is far more diversified than the pie chart on the left (a typical balanced portfolio that has a 60 percent stock allocation and a 40 percent bond allocation). The 7Twelve portfolio utilizes 12 different mutual funds to gain exposure to a wide variety of investable asset classes. The typical "balanced" portfolio utilizes only U.S. stock and U.S. bonds. As will be shown in this book, the broadly diversified 7Twelve portfolio provides better performance with less risk than the typical two-asset balanced portfolio.

Throughout this book, the words "stock" and "equity" will be used interchangeably. A stock mutual fund is the same as an equity mutual fund. Likewise, bonds can also be referred to as fixed income products. So a bond mutual fund might also be called a fixed income fund. Of course, there are many different kinds of stock funds and many varieties of bond funds.

## Salsa Anyone?

The 7Twelve portfolio is a recipe for combining 12 asset classes that optimizes performance and minimizes risk. It's not complicated, but it does require more asset classes than typically used. It's like making salsa with 12 ingredients instead of salsa with just two ingredients. Salsa with two ingredients won't cut it.

Just as new recipes often call for unfamiliar ingredients, the 7Twelve portfolio recipe will integrate investment asset classes that may seem exotic. Remember that some recipes call for ingredients that we would never eat individually (say, Tabasco sauce). However, when combined with other ingredients the exotic ingredient is magically integrated in a way that enhances the overall dish . . . or portfolio.

It is the diversity of the ingredients that makes salsa taste great. It's just hard to imagine great salsa that has only two ingredients. Even if you use the best tomatoes and onions available, having only two ingredients will not produce great salsa. How about using a wide variety of tomatoes and a wide variety of onions? Nope, doesn't solve the problem. Even though you have diversity within the two ingredients, you still have only two ingredients—and that ain't salsa.

The salsa metaphor describes the approach many investors (and mutual fund companies) use today when building what they claim to be a diversified portfolio. Here is a common approach: A stock mutual fund that contains 500 U.S. stocks is combined with a bond mutual fund that contains several hundred bonds. The resulting portfolio is referred to as a diversified balanced portfolio—the classic 60/40 model, with 60 percent of the portfolio allocated to large-cap U.S. stocks and 40 percent of the portfolio allocated to bonds.

With so many individual stocks and bonds, it appears that a diversified portfolio has been created. Wrong. No matter how much diversification there is within each ingredient, this supposedly diversified portfolio still has only two different ingredients (or asset classes): large-cap U.S. stock and U.S. bonds. Variety *within* specific asset classes is very important, but variety *among* asset classes is just as important—perhaps even more important.

Variety within an asset class represents "intra-asset" diversification, whereas variety among asset classes represents "inter-asset" diversification. Both forms of diversification are important. Nearly all mutual funds provide intra-asset

---

### 7TWELVE

The classic 60/40 balanced fund is 60 percent allocated to large-cap U.S. stocks and 40 percent allocated to bonds.

diversification. Very few provide inter-asset diversification. The 7Twelve portfolio provides both.

Very simply, more types of ingredients are needed to create a truly diversified portfolio (or great tasting salsa). Investment portfolios with genuine diversification have variety *within* and *among* asset classes, just like a good salsa that has a variety of tomatoes and onions *and* a wide array of other ingredients, such as peppers, lime juice, cilantro, salt, vinegar, and so on. Similarly, a great recipe for a diversified investment portfolio calls for 12 diversified ingredients, not just two.

In broad terms, the 7Twelve portfolio has an allocation of about 65 percent (66.6 percent to be exact) that is devoted to "Equity and Diversifying Funds" (U.S. stock, non–U.S. stock, real estate, resources) and about a 35 percent allocation (33.4 percent to be exact) to "Fixed Income Funds" (U.S. bonds, Non–U.S. bonds, and cash).

This two-thirds/one-third allocation pattern between stocks and bonds represents a classic "60/40 balanced" model, where 60 represents a 60 percent allocation to stocks (or equity investments) and 40 represents a 40 percent allocation to bonds (or fixed income). This general 60/40 allocation pattern is a useful starting point when building investment portfolios. However, the 7Twelve portfolio represents a much-needed diversification "upgrade" to the generic 60/40 model. In fact, the 7Twelve portfolio will be compared to the classic 60/40 portfolio throughout this entire book.

The seven core asset classes in the 7Twelve portfolio include U.S. stock, non–U.S. stock, real estate, resources, U.S. bonds, non–U.S. bonds, and cash. Underneath the seven core asset categories are 12 specific mutual funds. You can also use exchange-traded funds (ETFs) instead of mutual funds. An exchange traded fund is a mutual fund that trades like a stock.

## 7TWELVE

The seven core asset classes in the 7Twelve portfolio include U.S. stock, non–U.S. stock, real estate, resources, U.S. bonds, non–U.S. bonds, and cash.

The 12 different mutual funds represent the specific ingredients in the 7Twelve recipe. Let's take a look at the ingredients in first four broad asset classes, namely, U.S. stock, non–U.S. stock, real estate, and resources.

The first asset class to examine is U.S. stock. U.S. stock is often considered to be the "core" of many investment portfolios.

## U.S. Stock

| U.S. Stock | Non-U.S. Stock | Real Estate | Resources | U.S. Bonds | Non-U.S. Bonds | Cash |
|---|---|---|---|---|---|---|
| Large Companies | Developed Companies | Real Estate | Natural Resources | Aggregate Bonds | International Bonds | U.S. Cash |
| Medium-sized Companies | Emerging Companies | | Commodities | Inflation-Protected Bonds | | |
| Small Companies | | | | | | |

The 7Twelve portfolio utilizes three specific mutual funds in the U.S. stock asset class:

- Large-cap companies
- Midcap companies
- Small-cap companies

Each mutual fund has an 8.33 percent weighting (or allocation) in the 7Twelve portfolio; thus the U.S. stock "asset class" has a total allocation of about 25 percent in the 7Twelve portfolio—which is the largest allocation to any of the seven core asset categories. In other words, the 7Twelve portfolio's largest single commitment is to the U.S. stock asset class.

Let's talk first about large-cap U.S. stock, the first mutual fund in the U.S. stock asset class. Examples of large-cap U.S. stock (i.e., companies) are ExxonMobil, Microsoft, General Electric, Procter & Gamble, Johnson & Johnson, and the list goes on. Companies are classified as large cap (or mid-cap or small cap) based on their market capitalization (or "cap"), which is simply the current price of their stock multiplied by the number of shares of their stock that have been sold to investors. Large-cap stocks have a market cap of something over $8 billion. Small-cap stocks are market cap below about $1.5 billion. Midcap stocks are in between. These market cap boundaries are flexible, but these figures are general guidelines.

A well-known collection of large-cap U.S. companies is the Standard & Poor's 500 Index (or S&P 500). There are dozens of mutual funds that mimic the S&P 500 Index. Such funds are referred to as "index" funds, and index funds can mimic any index they choose. The most popular index to mimic is the S&P 500 Index. Funds that attempt to replicate the performance of the S&P 500 Index are referred to as *S&P 500 Index funds* (weird, huh?). More generally, they are simply referred to as *index funds*. But it's important to remember that there are other indexes that can be replicated by "index" funds. (This may come as a shock to the good folks at Standard & Poor's.)

Investing in the S&P 500 Index (by selecting an index fund) is a logical and appropriate way to invest in large-cap U.S. stock. Other large-cap U.S. stock indexes include the Russell 1000 Index or the Morgan Stanley U.S. Broad Market Index. Each of these indexes is investable via an appropriate index fund that has been chosen to mimic that particular index.

Let's assume an investor chooses to invest in an index fund that mimics the S&P 500 Index. The good news is that the investor has instant diversification across 500 large-cap U.S.

stocks. But that's all they have—a diversified fund that invests in only one specific subasset class, namely, large-cap U.S. stock. Our diversified portfolio recipe calls for 12 ingredients—there are eleven other ingredients missing.

Creating an investment portfolio by using only one mutual fund (using an S&P 500 Index fund, for example) would be comparable to making salsa using tomatoes only. However, being clever, you diversify and use five (or 500!) kinds of tomatoes. Sure, you have diversification among tomatoes, but diversified tomatoes doesn't create salsa! You need salt, cilantro, onions, peppers . . . and whatever else turns you on.

What I'm describing here represents a very common misunderstanding of diversification. Many investors believe they are diversified if they have a mutual fund that includes 500 different large-cap U.S. stocks. True, they have a diversified mutual fund. But it represents diversification only within one specific investment category, and there are many investment categories needed within a diversified portfolio.

The 7Twelve recipe creates a diversified portfolio using diversified individual ingredients (actual mutual funds). A mutual fund that mimics the S&P 500 Index represents only one diversified ingredient within a broadly diversified multi-asset portfolio. If we're making salsa, we need more than tomatoes. If we're making a diversified portfolio, we need more than 500 large-cap U.S. stocks. As of late 2009, there were about 750 large-cap stocks in the U.S. stock market (using data from Morningstar Principia).

There are two additional mutual funds we need to obtain to complete the U.S. stock category, namely, a mutual fund that invests in midcap U.S. stocks and a mutual fund that invests specifically in small-cap U.S. stocks.

Midsized and small U.S. companies are not as well known but often have more growth potential than large-cap U.S. companies. Think of large-cap U.S. stocks as adults, midcap

U.S. stocks as teenagers, and small-cap U.S. stocks as children. Children have the most growth potential, but they also present more risk (use your imagination here). Teenagers also have growth potential but also present more risk than most adults (no imagination needed here).

Examples of midcap U.S. stocks are Ross Stores ("Do these Bermuda shorts make me look skinny?"), Chipotle Mexican Grill ("Three cheesy encharitos to go, please!"), Aeropostale (a retailer of casual clothing, but as my children will confirm I'm waaaay too old to go there), and Kansas City Southern (look both ways before you cross the tracks). According to Morningstar, there were about 980 midcap U.S. companies in late 2009. The performance of midcap U.S. stock is captured by several different indexes: S&P Midcap 400 Index, Russell Midcap Index, Morningstar Mid Core Index, and others. Mutual funds and ETFs that mimic the various midcap indexes are widely available.

Small-cap U.S. companies are like small fish in the ocean: abundant, but at risk. If, however, they make it past puberty they stand a chance of becoming a midcap fish, or possibly even a big fish. That's where the growth potential comes from. Investors love to invest in little fish that become big fish.

The obvious challenge is selecting the little companies that will survive. As of late 2009, there were about 5,100 small-cap stocks in the U.S. market (at least that many were included in the Morningstar database). Many of those companies won't exist two years later. Therefore, the only sane way to invest in small-cap stock (or any stock for that matter) is by investing in a mutual fund that purchases hundreds or thousands of small companies (or midcap stock or large-cap stock). This approach represents the central tenet of diversification: spread risk across multiple investments. It is a principle that applies to mutual funds as well as portfolios that utilize multiple mutual funds—such as the 7Twelve portfolio.

Examples of small-cap U.S. companies (as of late 2009) include 99¢ Only Stores ("Hey, why is this yo-yo $1.50?"), ACME United Corporation (I believe they have a contract with Wiley Coyote), Caribou Coffee Company ("Ah, mousse latte, please"), and Great Wolf Resorts ("A warm welcome to red-heads"). As you can see, small-cap U.S. companies tend to be names we're not exactly familiar with yet . . . and possibly never will be.

There are a number of U.S. small-cap stock indexes that attempt to capture the aggregate performance of small-cap U.S. companies. Examples are the Russell 2000 Index, S&P Smallcap 600 Index, or Dow Jones U.S. Smallcap Index. There are a number of mutual funds and ETFs that mimic these (and other) small-cap stock indexes.

We've now reviewed the three mutual funds that comprise the U.S. stock "ingredients" in the 7Twelve portfolio.

The annual returns for each U.S. stock "ingredient" over the past 10 years are listed in Table 1.1. Also shown is the 10-year annualized percentage return (which is not a simple average of the 10 annual returns, but rather a compounded average annualized return or, in technical terms, the geometric mean return), the 10-year standard deviation of return (a measure of the volatility in the annual returns, and therefore a measure of risk), and the growth of $10,000 over the full 10-year period from January 1, 2000, to December 31, 2009.

A higher standard deviation of return indicates higher risk—more on that issue later. The standard deviation shown here is based on annual returns; whereas the standard deviation reported by Morningstar is based on monthly returns. As a result, they will be different. Either calculation is correct. The main thing is to stay consistent and not compare annual standard deviation of return against monthly standard deviation of return.

**Table 1.1   Annual Returns of the U.S. Stock Ingredients**

| Year | Large-cap U.S. Stock (%) | Midcap U.S. Stock (%) | Small-cap U.S. Stock (%) |
|---|---|---|---|
| 2000 | −9.70 | 17.38 | 21.88 |
| 2001 | −11.86 | −0.90 | 13.70 |
| 2002 | −21.50 | −14.51 | −14.20 |
| 2003 | 28.16 | 35.26 | 37.19 |
| 2004 | 10.69 | 15.89 | 23.55 |
| 2005 | 4.86 | 12.51 | 6.18 |
| 2006 | 15.80 | 9.96 | 19.38 |
| 2007 | 5.12 | 7.20 | −6.94 |
| 2008 | −36.70 | −36.39 | −32.19 |
| 2009 | 26.32 | 37.52 | 30.93 |
| 10-Year Average Annualized Return | **−1.00** | **6.10** | **7.76** |
| 10-Year Standard Deviation of Annual Returns | **20.90** | **21.97** | **21.78** |
| 10-Year Growth of $10,000 | **$9,047** | **$18,083** | **$21,106** |

Next, we'll review non–U.S. stock, the second asset class category in the 7Twelve recipe.

## Non–U.S. Stock

*7 Core Asset Classes*

| U.S. Stock | Non-U.S. Stock | Real Estate | Resources | U.S. Bonds | Non-U.S. Bonds | Cash |
|---|---|---|---|---|---|---|
| Large Companies | Developed Companies | Real Estate | Natural Resources | Aggregate Bonds | International Bonds | U.S. Cash |
| Medium-sized Companies | Emerging Companies | | Commodities | Inflation-Protected Bonds | | |
| Small Companies | | | | | | |

Got a Nokia cell phone? How about a Sony flat-screen TV? Maybe you drive a Hyundai? Nokia is a Finnish corporation,

Japan is home to Sony, and Hyundai is headquartered in South Korea.

There are two mutual funds utilized in the 7Twelve portfolio that invest specifically in non–U.S. stock. Investing in companies outside the United States is central to a well-diversified portfolio. (And if you live in Madrid, then investing in companies outside Spain is central to a well-diversified portfolio.) In short, investing in stock markets all over the world is the goal of a well-diversified portfolio. The 7Twelve portfolio devotes two slots (mutual funds) to non–U.S. stock, representing almost 17 percent of the total 7Twelve model.

Two specific mutual funds accomplish this goal of diversifying outside the U.S. The first mutual fund focuses on larger companies in non–U.S. countries such as Britain, Germany, France, Italy, Australia, Japan, Korea, Brazil, Sweden, Canada, Finland, and others. Well-known companies from developed non–U.S. countries include Nestle, GlaxoSmithKline, Mitsubushi, Toyota, British Petroleum, Novartis, Nokia, Credit Suisse, Honda, Samsung Electronics, France Telecom, America Movil, Deutsche Bank, and many others. According to the Morningstar database, there were about 400 large non–U.S. companies as of late 2009. The most popular market benchmark for gauging the performance on developed non–U.S. stocks is the Morgan Stanley Capital International Europe, Asia, and Far East Index (or EAFE Index).

The second mutual fund in the non–U.S. stock category invests in medium and small non–U.S. companies from a variety of countries. Examples of smaller non–U.S. stocks are Air France, Electrolux, Bank of Ireland, Norsk Hydro, Telecom Corporation of New Zealand, Peugeot, Royal Caribbean Cruises, and thousands of others. In fact, there were over 5,300 medium and small non–U.S. companies in the Morningstar database as of late 2009.

The annual returns over the past 10 years for the two non–U.S. stock funds in the 7Twelve portfolio are listed in Table 1.2.

One of the virtues of investing in non–U.S. stock is that the performance of international stock mutual funds is different from the performance of U.S. stock mutual funds. In other words, non–U.S. stock adds diversity to a portfolio— and diversity is a vitally important attribute of a portfolio. However, as will be shown, the performance of non–U.S. stocks has become increasingly similar to the performance of U.S. stocks, and this requires the use of additional assets in a portfolio. This is the problem that the multi-asset 7Twelve portfolio solves.

The next ingredient in the 7Twelve recipe is real estate.

**Table 1.2    Annual Returns of the Non–U.S. Stock Ingredients**

| Year | Non–U.S. Stock (%) | Emerging Non–U.S. Stock (%) |
| --- | --- | --- |
| 2000 | −14.46 | −27.45 |
| 2001 | −21.71 | −2.73 |
| 2002 | −15.43 | −7.29 |
| 2003 | 39.71 | 57.88 |
| 2004 | 18.94 | 26.31 |
| 2005 | 13.35 | 32.25 |
| 2006 | 25.79 | 29.20 |
| 2007 | 9.94 | 37.32 |
| 2008 | −41.01 | −52.46 |
| 2009 | 26.88 | 76.32 |
| 10-Year Average Annualized Return | **1.00** | **9.88** |
| 10-Year Standard Deviation of Annual Returns | **25.87** | **39.23** |
| 10-Year Growth of $10,000 | **$11,041** | **$25,657** |

# Real Estate

| U.S. Stock | Non-U.S. Stock | Real Estate | Resources | U.S. Bonds | Non-U.S. Bonds | Cash |
|---|---|---|---|---|---|---|
| Large Companies | Developed Companies | Real Estate | Natural Resources | Aggregate Bonds | International Bonds | U.S. Cash |
| Medium-sized Companies | Emerging Companies | | Commodities | Inflation-Protected Bonds | | |
| Small Companies | | | | | | |

"Investing in real estate, what's with that . . . I own a house, isn't that enough?" Nope, it's not enough. There are two reasons why. First, owning a house is a direct investment in real estate (which is great), but it's not a diversified real estate investment. It's only one house. Diversification is central to everything we do as investors.

Second, most real estate mutual funds invest in companies that are broadly related to real estate as an industry. The funds are not simply buying a bunch of houses. A real estate–based mutual fund invests in the stock of what are referred to as "real estate investment trusts," or REITs. Examples of companies (i.e., stocks) that a REIT fund invests in include Public Storage, Host Hotels and Resorts, Duke Realty Corporation, AvalonBay Communities, LaSalle Hotel Properties, Simon Property Group, and many others.

Some real estate mutual funds also invest in non–U.S. REITs, such as British Land Company, Mitsui Fudosan Company, or Brookfield Asset Management in Canada. A well-known barometer of the performance of real estate investment trusts is the Dow Jones U.S. Real Estate Index.

As you can see, investing in a REIT fund is actually a very different type of investment than simply purchasing a home. In fact, real estate investment trust mutual funds can be thought of as a diversifying investment because real

**Table 1.3   Annual Returns of Real Estate**

| Year | Real Estate (%) |
|---|---|
| 2000 | 26.46 |
| 2001 | 12.45 |
| 2002 | 3.85 |
| 2003 | 35.77 |
| 2004 | 30.87 |
| 2005 | 11.99 |
| 2006 | 35.05 |
| 2007 | −16.51 |
| 2008 | −36.91 |
| 2009 | 30.11 |
| 10-Year Average Annualized Return | **10.52** |
| 10-Year Standard Deviation of Annual Returns | **24.14** |
| 10-Year Growth of $10,000 | **$27,198** |

estate funds behave differently than traditional stock mutual funds.

The annual performance of real estate (via a real estate investment trust mutual fund) is shown in Table 1.3.

# Resources

| U.S. Stock | Non-U.S. Stock | Real Estate | Resources | U.S. Bonds | Non-U.S. Bonds | Cash |
|---|---|---|---|---|---|---|
| Large Companies | Developed Companies | Real Estate | Natural Resources | Aggregate Bonds | International Bonds | U.S. Cash |
| Medium-sized Companies | Emerging Companies | | Commodities | Inflation-Protected Bonds | | |
| Small Companies | | | | | | |

The asset class of "resources" requires two separate mutual funds, one that invests in natural resources companies (companies that mine, refine, process, and transport commodities) and another fund that invests in actual commodities (cattle, precious and industrial metals, wheat, corn, cotton, and so on).

Examples of natural resource companies are Schlumberger (a French oil and gas exploration company), Chevron, Overseas Shipholding Group, Sealed Air Corporation, Packaging Corporation of America, Barrick Gold Corporation, Newmont Mining, ConocoPhillips, Southern Union Company, Alcoa, Weyerhaeuser, and many others.

Investing in actual commodities is not like purchasing stock in a company. It involves the purchase of futures contracts for commodities such as heating oil, crude oil, soybeans, corn, wheat, aluminum, cattle, coffee, sugar, cotton, gold, natural gas, zinc, silver, nickel, lean hogs, and others. Hey, everybody should own lean hogs in their portfolio! "Lean" hogs . . . is that a cruel joke?

Investing in commodities is more complicated than simply investing in stock of a corporation, which is why investing in commodities should be accomplished by purchasing a commodities-based mutual fund (or exchange-traded fund). The historical performance of investing in commodities makes it a very attractive ingredient in a well diversified portfolio. There are several major indexes that track commodities. The most well known is the S&P Goldman Sachs Commodity Index. Both of these categories are also referred to as portfolio diversifiers because they behave differently than traditional stock mutual funds.

We have now reviewed eight of the 12 subassets (mutual funds) in the 7Twelve portfolio. Five of the eight funds are categorized as "equity" funds (equity is another name for stock). Among those five funds, three focus on U.S. stocks and the other two invest in non–U.S. stocks. The remaining three funds are categorized as "diversifying" assets (one fund that invests in the "Real Estate" asset class and two funds that invest in the "Resources" asset class).

It's not uncommon to hear people refer to real estate mutual funds, natural resources mutual funds, and commodities mutual funds as "alternative" asset classes. It's actually an odd expression because real estate, natural resources, and commodities should not be thought of as alternatives to traditional stock mutual funds. Rather, they should be included in a diversified portfolio in conjunction with traditional stock mutual funds. In fact, "alternative assets" such as real estate, natural resources, and commodities tend to complement and enhance stock funds because of their low correlation to the performance pattern of traditional stock funds. I will discuss the issue of "correlation" in Chapter 5.

The annual returns of the two "resources" ingredients in the 7Twelve portfolio are listed in Table 1.4.

We now turn our attention to the four fixed income components of the 7Twelve portfolio. Each of the four fixed income components is weighted at 8.33 percent of the

**Table 1.4    Annual Returns of the Resources Ingredients**

| Year | Resources (%) | Commodities (%) |
|------|---------------|-----------------|
| 2000 | 15.24 | 24.43 |
| 2001 | −16.00 | −8.68 |
| 2002 | −13.49 | 24.56 |
| 2003 | 33.37 | 25.84 |
| 2004 | 24.38 | 37.15 |
| 2005 | 35.96 | 30.87 |
| 2006 | 16.40 | 16.02 |
| 2007 | 33.45 | 31.50 |
| 2008 | −42.88 | −31.73 |
| 2009 | 37.11 | 16.18 |
| 10-Year Average Annualized Return | **8.67** | **14.49** |
| 10-Year Standard Deviation of Annual Returns | **27.38** | **21.17** |
| 10-Year Growth of $10,000 | **$22,975** | **$38,683** |

overall portfolio. The first fixed income asset class is U.S. Bonds. The term "fixed income" refers to bonds and cash, whereas the term "equity" refers to stocks. Cash is a term that refers to money market accounts, money market mutual funds, or a certificate of deposit.

## U.S. Bonds

| U.S. Stock | Non-U.S. Stock | Real Estate | Resources | U.S. Bonds | Non-U.S. Bonds | Cash |
|---|---|---|---|---|---|---|
| Large Companies | Developed Companies | Real Estate | Natural Resources | Aggregate Bonds | International Bonds | U.S. Cash |
| Medium-sized Companies | Emerging Companies | | Commodities | Inflation-Protected Bonds | | |
| Small Companies | | | | | | |

Bonds are different than stock. Stock in a company never expires (at least in theory) and stock represents ownership in the company. If you buy stock in Southwest Airlines, you are an owner—albeit a very small owner. Bonds, on the other hand, have a termination date. At that date, the bond expires and the person holding the bond receives $1,000. In the years prior to its expiration, bonds pay interest to the holder of the bond. A person who purchases a Southwest Airlines bond does not have any ownership interest in Southwest. Rather, they are essentially a lender to Southwest Airlines. That's my bonds 101 discussion.

The reason bonds are included in a portfolio is because they almost always have positive returns *and* the return pattern of bonds is quite different than the return patterns of stock. Remember, when building a portfolio, the goal is to combine investment assets that have very different return patterns.

Combining investments with different return patterns is how diversified portfolios are created. Think salsa here.

Investing in U.S. bonds can be achieved by selecting a bond mutual fund, specifically one that mimics a well-known bond index such as the Barclays Capital Aggregate Bond Index. This particular index invests in hundreds of different bonds. Diversification is important when investing in bonds, just as it is when investing in stocks. That's why bond mutual funds invest in hundreds of different bonds and stock mutual funds invest in hundreds (or even thousands) of different stocks.

The enemy of bonds is inflation. When prices increase (the inflation thing), the fixed amount of interest paid to bondholders becomes worth less. This problem is dealt with by the second U.S. bond asset: inflation-protected bonds. This type of bond is officially known as Treasury Inflation Protected Bonds, or TIPS. It is a relatively new class of U.S. bonds, having come into existence in the late 1990s.

Here's what the government website TreasuryDirect (www.treasurydirect.gov) has to say about TIPS: "Treasury Inflation-Protected Securities, or TIPS, provide protection against inflation. The principal of a TIPS increases with inflation and decreases with deflation, as measured by the Consumer Price Index. When a TIPS matures, you are paid the adjusted principal or original principal, whichever is greater."

That's all good. The bottom line is that we want some bonds in the portfolio that can defend themselves against inflation. Purchasing a TIPS mutual fund accomplishes this goal. A well-known TIPS benchmark is the Barclays Capital U.S. Treasury Inflation-Protected Securities Index ... Just kind of rolls off the tongue doesn't it?

Shown in Table 1.5 are the annual returns of the two U.S. bond funds included in the 7Twelve portfolio.

**Table 1.5   Annual Returns of the U.S. Bond Ingredients**

| Year | U.S. Bonds (%) | TIPS (%) |
|---|---|---|
| 2000 | 11.49 | 12.95 |
| 2001 | 8.31 | 7.68 |
| 2002 | 10.12 | 16.33 |
| 2003 | 3.98 | 8.18 |
| 2004 | 4.21 | 8.29 |
| 2005 | 2.31 | 2.52 |
| 2006 | 4.21 | 0.29 |
| 2007 | 6.84 | 11.93 |
| 2008 | 8.41 | −0.53 |
| 2009 | 3.57 | 8.96 |
| 10-Year Average Annualized Return | **6.30** | **7.53** |
| 10-Year Standard Deviation of Annual Returns | **3.12** | **5.49** |
| 10-Year Growth of $10,000 | **$18,430** | **$20,674** |

## Non–U.S. Bonds

| U.S. Stock | Non-U.S. Stock | Real Estate | Resources | U.S. Bonds | Non-U.S. Bonds | Cash |
|---|---|---|---|---|---|---|
| Large Companies | Developed Companies | Real Estate | Natural Resources | Aggregate Bonds | International Bonds | U.S. Cash |
| Medium-sized Companies | Emerging Companies | | Commodities | Inflation-Protected Bonds | | |
| Small Companies | | | | | | |

Next in the fixed income arsenal is non–U.S. bonds. Investing in bonds outside the United States is just as important as investing in bonds inside the U.S. Global fixed income diversification is achieved by adding an international bond fund to the 7Twelve portfolio. International bond mutual funds invest in bonds from a wide variety of non–U.S. countries, such as the United Kingdom, Japan, Germany, Greece, Sweden, Canada, Spain, Austria, South Africa, Mexico, Poland, Taiwan,

**Table 1.6   Annual Returns of Non–U.S. Bonds**

| Year | International Bonds (%) |
| --- | --- |
| 2000 | −3.13 |
| 2001 | −3.41 |
| 2002 | 21.80 |
| 2003 | 18.78 |
| 2004 | 11.41 |
| 2005 | −8.18 |
| 2006 | 7.55 |
| 2007 | 10.06 |
| 2008 | 4.22 |
| 2009 | 5.43 |
| 10-Year Average Annualized Return | **6.06** |
| 10-Year Standard Deviation of Annual Returns | **9.64** |
| 10-Year Growth of $10,000 | **$18,011** |

and Gilroy. Caught ya! Gilroy is in California and holds the esteemed title of Garlic Capital of the World.

The annual returns of non–U.S. bonds are listed in Table 1.6.

## Cash

| U.S. Stock | Non-U.S. Stock | Real Estate | Resources | U.S. Bonds | Non-U.S. Bonds | Cash |
| --- | --- | --- | --- | --- | --- | --- |
| Large Companies | Developed Companies | Real Estate | Natural Resources | Aggregate Bonds | International Bonds | U.S. Cash |
| Medium-sized Companies | Emerging Companies | | Commodities | Inflation-Protected Bonds | | |
| Small Companies | | | | | | |

The final and fourth component of the fixed income group is cash. Good old U.S. Treasury bills. Cash isn't exciting, but it always provides a positive "nominal" return (nominal means that we ignore taxes and inflation). The practical way to add cash to a portfolio is to purchase a money market mutual fund, which provides a return very similar to Treasury

**Table 1.7   Annual Returns of Cash**

| Year | Cash (%) |
| --- | --- |
| 2000 | 6.29 |
| 2001 | 4.16 |
| 2002 | 1.65 |
| 2003 | 0.90 |
| 2004 | 1.11 |
| 2005 | 3.01 |
| 2006 | 4.88 |
| 2007 | 5.14 |
| 2008 | 2.77 |
| 2009 | 0.53 |
| 10-Year Average Annualized Return | **3.03** |
| 10-Year Standard Deviation of Annual Returns | **2.01** |
| 10-Year Growth of $10,000 | **$13,474** |

bills (or T-bills). Cash is a safe haven, and every portfolio needs several of those. Cash is a poor choice as a sole investment for the long run, due to lower returns, but is a wonderful portfolio component because it represents a safe haven at all times. After experiencing large losses in stocks in 2008, it should be self evident that every portfolio should have at least one safe haven asset. The annual returns of cash are shown in Table 1.7.

## The Complete Recipe

The 12 mutual funds in the 7Twelve portfolio are themselves diversified investment products. Many of the mutual funds contain hundreds of different stocks or bonds. Because the 7Twelve portfolio brings together so many diverse mutual funds, it contains more than 4,000 holdings (as shown in Table 1.8).

Importantly, the separate mutual funds all focus on different asset classes. As a result, redundancy among the thousands of underlying holdings in the 7Twelve portfolio has been minimized. This is vitally important because redundancy is of no

**Table 1.8  Total Number of Holdings in the 7Twelve Portfolio**

| Mutual Fund Category | Number of Holdings |
|---|---|
| Large-cap U.S. Stock | 501 |
| Midcap U.S. Stock | 400 |
| Small-cap U.S. Stock | 1,025 |
| Non–U.S. Developed Stock | 851 |
| Non–U.S. Emerging Stock | 778 |
| Real Estate | 99 |
| Natural Resources | 125 |
| Commodities | 27 |
| U.S. Bonds | 248 |
| Inflation-protected Bonds | 29 |
| Non–U.S. Bonds | 102 |
| Cash | — |
| **Total Holdings** | **$4,000+** |

---

## 7TWELVE

*Depth* of diversity is achieved within each mutual fund and *breadth* of diversity is achieved by investing in 12 different mutual funds that span across seven core asset classes

---

value in a portfolio. The 7Twelve portfolio provides diversification breadth and depth. *Depth* of diversity is achieved within each mutual fund and *breadth* of diversity is achieved by investing in 12 different mutual funds that span seven core asset classes.

How has the 7Twelve portfolio performed *as a portfolio?* Table 1.9 shows the annual returns of all 12 equally weighted funds from 2000 to 2009 (see the far right column). The performance of the 7Twelve portfolio in Table 1.9 assumes that all 12 ingredients were "rebalanced" at the end of each year (see Chapter 6 for more about rebalancing). The performance of the 7Twelve portfolio reported on my website (www.7TwelvePortfolio.com) assumes monthly rebalancing,

**Table 1.9 Annual Returns of the 7Twelve Portfolio**

| Year | Large-cap U.S. Stock (%) | Midcap U.S. Stock (%) | Small-cap U.S. Stock (%) | Non-U.S. Stock (%) | Emerging Non-U.S. Stock (%) | Real Estate (%) | Resources (%) | Commodities (%) | U.S. Bonds (%) | TIPS (%) | International Bonds (%) | Cash (%) | 7Twelve Portfolio (%) |
|---|---|---|---|---|---|---|---|---|---|---|---|---|---|
| 2000 | -9.70 | 17.38 | 21.88 | -14.46 | -27.45 | 26.46 | 15.24 | 24.43 | 11.49 | 12.95 | -3.13 | 6.29 | 6.78 |
| 2001 | -11.86 | -0.90 | 13.70 | -21.71 | -2.73 | 12.45 | -16.00 | -8.68 | 8.31 | 7.68 | -3.41 | 4.16 | -1.58 |
| 2002 | -21.50 | -14.51 | -14.20 | -15.43 | -7.29 | 3.85 | -13.49 | 24.56 | 10.12 | 16.33 | 21.80 | 1.65 | -0.68 |
| 2003 | 28.16 | 35.26 | 37.19 | 39.71 | 57.88 | 35.77 | 33.37 | 25.84 | 3.98 | 8.18 | 18.78 | 0.90 | 27.08 |
| 2004 | 10.69 | 15.89 | 23.55 | 18.94 | 26.31 | 30.87 | 24.38 | 37.15 | 4.21 | 8.29 | 11.41 | 1.11 | 17.73 |
| 2005 | 4.86 | 12.51 | 6.18 | 13.35 | 32.25 | 11.99 | 35.96 | 30.87 | 2.31 | 2.52 | -8.18 | 3.01 | 12.30 |
| 2006 | 15.80 | 9.96 | 19.38 | 25.79 | 29.20 | 35.05 | 16.40 | 16.02 | 4.21 | 0.29 | 7.55 | 4.88 | 15.38 |
| 2007 | 5.12 | 7.20 | -6.94 | 9.94 | 37.32 | -16.51 | 33.45 | 31.50 | 6.84 | 11.93 | 10.06 | 5.14 | 11.25 |
| 2008 | -36.70 | -36.39 | -32.19 | -41.01 | -52.46 | -36.91 | -42.88 | -31.73 | 8.41 | -0.53 | 4.22 | 2.77 | -24.62 |
| 2009 | 26.32 | 37.52 | 30.93 | 26.88 | 76.32 | 30.11 | 37.11 | 16.18 | 3.57 | 8.96 | 5.43 | 0.53 | 24.99 |
| 10-Year Average Annualized Return | -1.00 | 6.10 | 7.76 | 1.00 | 9.88 | 10.52 | 8.67 | 14.49 | 6.30 | 7.53 | 6.06 | 3.03 | 7.81 |
| 10-Year Standard Deviation of Annual Returns | 20.90 | 21.97 | 21.78 | 25.87 | 39.23 | 24.14 | 27.38 | 21.17 | 3.12 | 5.49 | 9.64 | 2.01 | 15.11 |
| 10-Year Growth of $10,000 | $9,047 | $18,083 | $21,106 | $11,041 | $25,657 | $27,198 | $22,975 | $38,683 | $18,430 | $20,674 | $18,011 | $13,474 | $21,212 |

so you'll notice slight differences in the historical figures. I provide 7Twelve portfolio performance updates each month hence the need to assume monthly rebalancing on the website.

However, there is also downloadable software (an Excel template) on my website that allows you to compare other funds and/or portfolios against the 7Twelve portfolio. The template assumes annual rebalancing so that it coincides with the performance reported in this book. By the way, annual rebalancing tends to produce slightly better performance than monthly rebalancing.

The 7Twelve portfolio had a 10-year annualized return of 7.81 percent and a 10-year standard deviation of annual returns of 15.11 percent. For comparison, the large-cap U.S. stock ingredient (the S&P 500 Index) had a 10-year annualized return of -1.00 percent and a standard deviation of return of 20.90 percent. The 7Twelve portfolio had much higher return with less risk. A $10,000 investment in the S&P 500 Index on January 1, 2000, was worth $9,047 by December 31, 2009. Alternatively, $10,000 invested in the 7Twelve portfolio was worth $21,212 by the end of 2009.

During the tough years of 2000 to 2002, when most of the stock funds had sizeable negative returns, the 7Twelve portfolio performed wonderfully. In the subsequent rebound years of 2003–2007, the 7Twelve portfolio delivered returns that were comparable to or better than the S&P 500 (the "Large-cap U.S. Stock" ingredient).

In 2008, even broad diversification didn't sidestep the mayhem of the markets. Some may suggest that because of what happened in 2008, diversification doesn't work. That is incorrect for at least two reasons. First, the performance of a broadly diversified portfolio (the 7Twelve) from 2000–2007 and 2009 shows that diversification does work well in minimizing downside without missing upside.

Second, if a person doesn't diversify, what is his or her alternative? The only alternative would be to have perfect foresight and choose the asset that will perform best going forward. Last time I checked, the magicians have left the castle. Perfect foresight is not a viable portfolio strategy. Diversification is the only viable approach. The year 2008 did not change that. With the ingredients and the performance of the 7Twelve portfolio outlined, Chapter 2 reviews the guidelines of the recipe that determine how the 7Twelve portfolio is assembled and managed.

# LINING UP THE INGREDIENTS

The 7Twelve portfolio is a completely strategic portfolio design. Strategic portfolios are built and managed by following preset guidelines that are not affected by whim, opinion, or market gyrations. A strategic portfolio is often viewed as a more "passive" approach to investing because it does not imply, or rely upon, skill or market timing. Rather, a strategic portfolio relies upon commitment to the recipe and adherence to the preset guidelines. Strategic portfolios set a course and follow it.

The opposite of strategic is tactical. A tactical portfolio is much more dependent on skill, opinion, and luck. A tactical portfolio has a flexible set of guidelines that can change based on market conditions or opinions of the manager. A tactical portfolio may change course at any time.

As a strategic portfolio, the 7Twelve recipe follows three simple guidelines:

1. Select 12 different "ingredients" or mutual funds
2. Equally weight the ingredients
3. Rebalance periodically

Each of the 12 mutual funds in the 7Twelve portfolio is assigned an equal allocation of 8.33 percent. The 7Twelve portfolio includes eight equity-based mutual funds that create an overall equity (stock) allocation of approximately 65 percent equity (66.6 percent to be exact). Four fixed income funds create a total fixed income (bond) allocation of about 35 percent (33.3 percent to be precise).

With a 65 percent equity/35 percent fixed income asset allocation model, the 7Twelve can be categorized as a "balanced" portfolio because it has an overall asset allocation model that conforms to the general 60 percent stock/40 percent bond template. However, the 7Twelve portfolio is much more diversified than the typical 60/40 balanced portfolio.

**The 7Twelve Portfolio Recipe**

| Equity 65% of Portfolio Four Broad Asset Categories Eight Specific Stock or Diversifying Mutual Funds | | | | Fixed Income 35% of Portfolio Three Broad Asset Categories Four Specific Bond or Cash Mutual Funds | | |
|---|---|---|---|---|---|---|
| **U.S. Stock** | **Non-U.S. Stock** | **Real Estate** | **Resources** | **U.S. Bonds** | **Non-U.S. Bonds** | **Cash** |
| Large Companies | Developed Markets | Real Estate | Natural Resources | U.S. Aggregate Bonds | International Bonds | U.S. Cash |
| Medium-sized Companies | Emerging Markets | | Commodities | Inflation-Protected Bonds | | |
| Small Companies | | | | | | |

The 7Twelve design and asset allocation model does not change based on market conditions. The performance of the 7Twelve is, of course, affected by the performance of its 12 underlying investments, but the recipe does not change based upon the behavior of investment markets. Some people refer to this type of portfolio design as a "passive" approach. It rewards investors who exercise patience in following the recipe and who do not attempt to "overmanage" the portfolio.

## 7TWELVE

The asset allocation of the 7Twelve Portfolio does not change based on market conditions. Some might refer to this as "passive" investing. I call it having a plan and following it!

Investment portfolios that are actively changing based on market conditions are referred to as tactical portfolios. Tactical portfolios ultimately rely upon the skill of the portfolio manager to react appropriately to changing market conditions. A tactical portfolio would, for example, be much less likely to equally weight the ingredients of the portfolio. Moreover, a tactical portfolio will tend to overweight or underweight various portfolio components at the discretion of the portfolio manager. If the manager is correct, the portfolio wins. If wrong, the portfolio loses. It's all based on skill, and skill is actually very hard to find. Tactical portfolios are referred to as an "active" portfolio management paradigm.

If you want to test the 7Twelve philosophy, set up a competition between two portfolios. The first portfolio could be the "passive" multi-asset 7Twelve portfolio. The second could be a mutual fund that is actively managed and that relies upon tactical, market-timing skill. You will likely discover that a passive, multi-asset core is a better starting point. To keep each of the 12 mutual funds equally weighted at 8.33 percent of the total portfolio, rebalancing must occur on a periodic basis (monthly, quarterly, or annually). How often the 7Twelve portfolio is rebalanced is up to each individual investor or his or her financial advisor. More on the mechanics of rebalancing in Chapter 6.

A number of financial advisors around the country use the 7Twelve portfolio as the recipe for building their clients' portfolios. As the originator and developer (the "master chef," so to speak) of the 7Twelve portfolio recipe, I believe that its straightforward design and transparent logic is the most appealing aspect of it. You know what you have and you know how it works.

If an investment portfolio is hard to explain, it will be hard to understand. If it's hard to understand, most investors won't want to use it. Alternatively, if a portfolio has a straightforward rationale with transparent rules, it will be easy to explain and easy to understand. That's precisely why the 7Twelve portfolio is being utilized by several hundred financial advisors. Advisors and their clients can quickly perceive the design concepts and rules of the 7Twelve portfolio recipe. And we know how fast good recipes can travel.

## A Recipe That Goes Waaay Back

The origins of the 7Twelve recipe began years ago. Like most recipes, it was refined over a period of time.

The 7Twelve portfolio is the indirect result of more than 20 years of mutual fund research and analysis. I say "indirect" because I never set out to design a multi-asset portfolio. In the process of writing an article for the *Journal of Indexes* in 2007, I gathered and studied long-run performance data for seven major investment categories, or "asset classes." The seven major asset classes included in my original study were U.S. large-cap stock, U.S. small-cap stock, non–U.S. stock, U.S. real estate, commodities, U.S. bonds, and U.S. cash. The historical performance data began in 1970. This seven-asset portfolio was the forerunner to what is now known as the 7Twelve portfolio. The seven-asset portfolio represents a subset of the 7Twelve portfolio.

While analyzing the performance of these seven asset classes, I experimented with different asset allocation models, or mixtures, of the various asset classes. Much like a recipe, an asset allocation model determines how much of each asset class is included in an investment portfolio. I tinkered around with various models in which varying allocations of each of the seven asset classes was included in a hypothetical portfolio. Then I had a strange thought (not unusual for me). What if I simply built a portfolio with equal amounts of each of the seven assets? The idea was simple. Rather than attempting to guess the right mix (which is a "tactical" behavior), perhaps I should simply build a portfolio that allocates to each asset an equal portion.

The best part of this simple approach is that building a portfolio with equal allocations to seven major asset classes eliminates the reliance upon special forecasting skills or snazzy mathematical models to determine how much of each asset class to include and when to change the allocation recipe.

So I tried it. I built an equally weighted, seven-asset portfolio. Each of the seven assets (or indexes) was assigned an allocation of 14.29 percent (1/7th of the portfolio) and at the end of each year each asset was rebalanced back to 14.29 percent of the total portfolio. There were only three rules of the portfolio (which should look very familiar). The rules are transparent, straightforward, and exceptionally easy to implement:

1. Select seven different ingredients (in this case, indexes)
2. Equally weight the ingredients
3. Rebalance each ingredient systematically

The results were stunning. An equally weighted seven-asset portfolio provided excellent performance with substantially reduced risk compared to the performance of the individual ingredients (or assets) or in comparison to less diversified portfolios over a period of nearly 40 years. The best news is that the superior risk-adjusted performance was not the result of any special skill. Rather, it was produced by assembling a broadly diversified portfolio and assigning equal allocations to all the ingredients—and then rebalancing at systematic intervals.

Some have referred to this type of portfolio design as naïve. I take that as a compliment. A naïve portfolio is one that acknowledges at the outset that transparent rules, rather than special skills, drive the results of the portfolio. But there is another important aspect of a simple, rules-based portfolio design—namely, the issue of performance back-testing.

The performance of a rules-based portfolio can be back-tested with confidence because the performance is based upon rules that anyone can follow. Conversely, portfolios that rely upon special managerial skills and real-time portfolio adjustments cannot be back-tested with confidence unless there is an assumption that the portfolio manager (i.e., "guru") always made the right judgment call historically. I've not met that person yet . . . and I look under a lot of rocks.

## Getting Better and Better

The fundamental principles from my seven-asset portfolio research in the fall of 2007 have now evolved into the 7Twelve portfolio: a multi-asset portfolio that represents seven core asset classes but that is implemented by utilizing 12 underlying mutual funds. Again, the original seven asset classes from my 2007 model were U.S. large-cap stock, U.S. small-cap stock, non–U.S. stock, real estate, commodities, bonds, and cash. These seven were chosen because performance data back to 1970 was available.

The 7Twelve portfolio represents an evolution of my original seven-asset model. It also utilizes seven core asset categories, but with several modifications. The seven core asset categories in the 7Twelve portfolio are U.S. stock, non–U.S. stock, real estate, resources, U.S. bonds, non–U.S. bonds, and cash. In the U.S. stock asset category, there are three underlying funds: large-cap U.S. stock, midcap U.S. stock, and small-cap U.S. stock. In the non–U.S. stock asset category, there are two underlying funds: developed non–U.S. stock and emerging non–U.S. stock. There is one underlying fund in the real estate category. There are two underlying funds in the resources asset class: natural resources and commodities.

The 7Twelve portfolio has three fixed income asset classes: U.S. bonds, non–U.S. bonds, and cash. In the U.S. bonds asset classes, there are two underlying funds: U.S. aggregate bonds and inflation-protected bonds. The asset class of non–U.S. bonds has one underlying fund, as does the cash asset class.

The 7Twelve portfolio made its debut in the summer of 2008. Its design was not a reaction to the gyrations of the investment markets in 2008 because it was designed in late 2007. As a strategic portfolio, the 7Twelve does not change with the wind. Rather, it employs 12 sails to catch a variety of winds.

The 7Twelve portfolio can be the foundation of a preretirement accumulation portfolio or the core holding in a postretirement distribution portfolio. The 7Twelve can represent your entire portfolio, or it can be a major component within a larger portfolio. However it is utilized, the 7Twelve design represents a fully diversified multi-asset balanced portfolio. The word "balanced" is an established term that implies a mixture of stocks and bonds.

The ultimate goal of this book is to make straightforward and implementable what has become complex and confusing to many financial advisors and individual investors, namely, the construction of a broadly diversified investment portfolio. The 7Twelve portfolio relies upon strategic rules rather than reactionary tactical portfolio adjustments.

## 7TWELVE

The 7Twelve can represent your entire portfolio or it can be a major component within a larger portfolio.

In summary, the three key guidelines in the 7Twelve recipe are selecting 12 different ingredients (such as mutual funds), allocating your investment equally among all 12 funds, and rebalancing the 12 funds on a periodic basis, such as annually. Chapter 3 is devoted to a discussion of the most defining characteristic of the 7Twelve portfolio—broad diversification.

# THE MORE INGREDIENTS,
# THE BETTER

The 7Twelve portfolio is all about diversification. Diversification, in essence, is the art and science of combining
ingredients that are sufficiently different from each other that
the whole is greater than the sum of the parts. Think salsa
here. Salsa, as a finished product, is a whole lot better than just
eating the various ingredients by themselves. Good salsa is all
about diversification. Good portfolios are all about diversification too.

The benefits of diversification are not a new phenomenon. What is new is the wide variety of investment assets that
have become "investable" during the past several decades.
Asset classes (such as real estate and commodities) that were
once represented only by uninvestable indexes are now actual
investment products that any investor can utilize in his or her
portfolio. We can now build portfolios that are more diversified than ever before. "Why should we?" The answer is very
simple: risk reduction.

In the first portion of this chapter, we will look at three different ways of defining and measuring risk. We'll then explore
the benefits of diversification using the 7Twelve portfolio over

a 10-year period from 2000 to 2009. The latter portion of the chapter will demonstrate the benefits of diversification using my original seven-asset portfolio over the 40-year period from 1970 to 2009.

You'll recall that the original seven-asset portfolio is a subset of the 7Twelve portfolio that includes the seven assets that have performance histories back to 1970. The seven assets are large-cap U.S. stock, small-cap U.S. stock, non–U.S. developed stock, real estate, commodities, U.S. bonds, and cash. The 7Twelve portfolio cannot be evaluated over the 40-year period because some of the ingredients did not exist for the entire period, such as TIPS.

## Measuring Volatility and Risk

Portfolio diversification reduces portfolio risk. In the context of an investment portfolio, risk can be defined and measured in a number of different ways:

1. Volatility of return in the portfolio
2. Worst-case return
3. Frequency of portfolio loss

The first measurement we'll discuss is volatility of return (monthly, quarterly, or annually). Volatility of return is a common definition of risk, where less volatility is preferred. The typical measure of volatility is standard deviation of return,

---

### Take Note!

The 7Twelve portfolio has several ingredients that don't have a 40-year performance history. Therefore, throughout the book, I will be using the 7Twelve portfolio when I present 10-year analysis and the seven-asset portfolio when I present 40-year analysis, which represents a subset of the 7Twelve portfolio.

a statistical measure that is often reported alongside the mean (or average annualized) return. A mutual fund with a high standard deviation of return would be considered a high-risk fund. Standard deviation of return, though commonly reported, is the least useful measure of risk because it is very difficult to understand in real-world terms. For example, what level of standard deviation represents a maximum threshold? Ten percent? Twenty percent? Who knows? All we know is that a higher standard deviation of return means higher volatility, and higher volatility is often equated to higher risk.

Another definition of risk is worst-case return. For example, we might ask, "What is the worst-case return of a particular investment?" The worst-case return can be measured over any time frame. When measuring worst-case return, I prefer to examine worst-case return over three-year periods using cumulative percentage return rather than average annual return.

Either measure of worst-case performance is perfectly acceptable. Cumulative percentage return measures the total gain or loss from the start of the period to the end of the period (whether it be one year, three years, five years, and so on). On the other hand, average annual return is a measure of the gain or loss expressed as an average per year over the time period in question.

Cumulative return is a measure of how much an investor's actual account balance increased or declined over the entire three-year period. This calculation is a much more "real-world" measure of risk. I use three years because a one-year period is too short. For example, if we don't feel well on a particular day, we don't typically run to the doctor's office. However, after three days of not feeling well, we might be inclined to see our doctor.

A third definition of risk is how often an investment account has lost money over a specified time frame, or "How often is the account underwater?" The term "underwater" is used to describe an account that has a lower current balance than the starting balance. This measure of risk will also be calculated over rolling three-year periods. For example, in the 10-year period from 2000 to 2009, there were eight rolling three-year periods. The first period was from 2000 to 2002, the second period was from 2001 to 2003, and so on. Bottom line: However we choose to measure risk, the goal of a well-designed investment portfolio is to reduce portfolio risk. Diversification is the best weapon to reduce risk.

Lastly, there is one easy step for instantly reducing portfolio risk: Check your portfolio less often! Monitoring your investment portfolio on a daily basis is like checking the daily growth of a newly planted oak tree. Before long you might convince yourself that this tree simply isn't growing—and you'll cut it down. Just like trees, portfolios require time . . . and surprisingly little oversight. A tree that is planted correctly doesn't need much help. Just water it, leave it alone, and let it grow. Likewise, a well-designed portfolio—for the most part—needs to be left alone. Annual rebalancing, such as at the start or end of each year is usually all that is needed. Overmanagement adversely impacts far more portfolios than undermanagement.

By checking your portfolio less often, you will protect yourself from emotionally reacting to short-term market volatility "noise." Do yourself a huge favor and don't micromanage your investment portfolio.

## Diversification by Design

The 7Twelve portfolio is diversified by design. The recipe is all about achieving diversification. We'll now investigate how well the recipe has performed over the past 10 years and the past 40 years.

First, let's look at how it's performed over the past 10 years. The 12 ingredients in the 7Twelve portfolio recipe are listed in

**Table 3.1   10-Year Analysis Using 7Twelve Portfolio (2000–2009)**

| Ingredient | Underlying Benchmark Index |
|---|---|
| Large-cap U.S. Stock | S&P 500 Index |
| Midcap U.S. Stock | S&P Midcap 400 Index |
| Small-cap U.S. Value Stock | Russell 2000 Value Index |
| Non–U.S. Developed Stock | MSCI EAFE Index |
| Non–U.S. Emerging Stock | MSCI Emerging Markets Index |
| Real Estate | Dow Jones U.S. Select REIT Index |
| Natural Resources | Goldman Sachs Natural Resources Index |
| Commodities | Deutsche Bank Liquid Commodity Index |
| U.S. Bonds | Barclays Capital Aggregate Bond Index |
| Inflation Protected Bonds | Barclays Capital U.S. Treasury Inflation Note Index |
| Non–U.S. Bonds | Citibank WGBI Non–U.S. Dollar Index |
| Cash | Three-Month Treasury bill |

Table 3.1. Also shown in the table is the most common underlying "index" representing that particular ingredient (or asset class). An index is a benchmark portfolio that measures the performance of particular asset classes. Prominent index makers are Standard & Poor's, Dow Jones, Morgan Stanley, Russell, Barclays, and Citibank.

To assess the impact diversification has on risk reduction, I will compare and contrast the multi-asset 7Twelve portfolio against a one-fund portfolio and a two-fund portfolio over the past decade (from January 1, 2000, to December 31, 2009). The performance figures in Table 3.2 reflect the performance of actual funds, not raw indexes.

The single fund "portfolio" (portfolio is in quotes because the term "portfolio" implies more than one asset class, which the one-fund portfolio fails to achieve) is entirely committed to U.S. large-cap stock (the S&P 500 Index). The two-fund portfolio will be the classic 60/40 balanced model, which allocates 60 percent of the portfolio to U.S. large-cap stock and 40 percent to bonds.

As shown in Table 3.2, the 7Twelve portfolio was significantly less risky in every risk measure when compared to the

**Table 3.2   Risk and Performance of Portfolios over 10-Year Period (2000–2009)**

| | One Fund | Two Fund | 7Twelve Portfolio |
|---|---|---|---|
| | 100% Large-cap U.S. Stock (%) | 60% Large-cap U.S. Stock/40% U.S. Bonds (%) | 8.33% Equal Allocation Across 12 Funds (%) |
| **Risk Measures** | | | |
| Standard Deviation of Annual Returns (%) | 20.9 | 11.6 | 15.1 |
| Worst 3-Year Cumulative Loss (%) | −37.6 | −13.4 | −3.2 |
| Percent of Time Underwater (Eight 3-year rolling periods) | 50 | 25 | 13 |
| **Performance Measures** | | | |
| 10-Year Average Annual Return | −1.0 | 2.6 | 7.8 |
| Average Rolling 3-Year Return | 0.5 | 3.2 | 8.8 |

one-fund portfolio. The 7Twelve portfolio had a standard deviation of annual return of 15.1 percent compared to 20.9 percent in the one-fund portfolio.

However, of all the risk measures, standard deviation is the least useful. More important is protecting investors from large losses. An investment in only large-cap U.S. stock didn't do that. In fact, a 100 percent U.S. large-cap stock "portfolio" had a cumulative loss of −37.6 percent during its worst three-year period (2000–2002). By contrast, the worst three-year cumulative percentage loss for the 7Twelve portfolio was −3.2 percent (2006–2008). That's a huge difference.

During this particular ten-year period, the one-fund portfolio was underwater in 50 percent of the eight rolling three-year periods compared to 13 percent of the time for the 7Twelve portfolio.

Compared to the two-fund portfolio, the 7Twelve portfolio was less risky in two of the three risk measures. Despite having a slightly higher standard deviation of return (the least useful measure of risk), the 7Twelve portfolio had a much better worst-case three-year loss (−3.2 percent vs. −13.4 percent) and was underwater half as often (13 percent of the time vs. 25 percent of the time).

Understandably, reducing risk is not the only goal of a portfolio. Also reported in Table 3.2 is the performance (measured as a 10-year average return and as the average return over eight rolling three-year periods) for the one-fund portfolio, the two-fund portfolio, and the 7Twelve portfolio.

The 10-year average annual return between 2000 and 2009 for the one-fund portfolio (100 percent U.S. large-cap stock) was −1.0 percent, which makes it the second worst performance over a 10-year period for the S&P 500 Index since 1926. The worst 10-year period was 1999–2008.

A portfolio composed of 60 percent large-cap U.S. stock and 40 percent bonds (the traditional "balanced" portfolio) performed better, producing a 10-year average annual return of 2.6 percent. Best of all was the 7Twelve portfolio with a 10-year average return of 7.8 percent.

Not all investors are patient, and so a 10-year measure of performance may be too long. Table 3.2 also reports the average three-year return (over eight rolling three-year periods between 2000 and 2009) for each of the three portfolios. The 7Twelve portfolio dominated. The average three-year return was 8.8 percent for the 7Twelve portfolio—which was dramatically higher than the 0.5 percent average for the one-fund portfolio and 3.2 percent average for the two-fund portfolio.

The average 10-year annualized return for each of the three portfolios, as well as the worst three-year cumulative percentage return, is shown graphically in Figure 3.1.

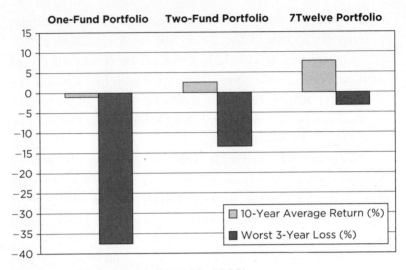

**Figure 3.1  10-Year Period (2000–2009)**

We have arrived at a really important observation. There is a significant benefit—both in terms of risk *and* return—when moving from a one-fund portfolio to a two-fund portfolio. Doing so reduced risk and improved performance. This is the essential idea behind diversification. But too many investors stop there, at a two-fund portfolio. They don't continue to diversify.

As shown in Figure 3.1, building an even more diversified portfolio that employs 12 different mutual funds (rather than just two funds) reduced risk and improved performance. Recall that this performance advantage took place during one of the worst 10-year periods in U.S. stock market history.

Let's now look at 40-year results using a seven-asset portfolio. Recall that the 7Twelve portfolio contains several ingredients that don't have a 40-year history, such as TIPS and international bonds. In order to test the 40-year performance of diversification, I will use seven of the 12 asset classes that have a 40-year performance history.

First, let's look at performance over the past 40 years. This 40-year analysis of the benefits of diversification covers the period from January 1, 1970, to December 31, 2009, and includes seven core asset classes: large-cap U.S. stock, small-cap U.S. stock, non–U.S. stock, U.S. bonds, cash, real estate, and commodities. This seven-asset portfolio represents a subset of the 7Twelve portfolio.

The seven asset classes are listed in Table 3.3. Each asset class is represented by an underlying index or combination of indexes if one index did not have a full 40-year performance history.

## Take Note!

Technical note for data geeks: The historical performance of the seven-asset portfolio is based on the annual returns of the underlying indexes, whereas the performance of the 7Twelve portfolio is based on the performance of actual mutual funds (specifically exchange-traded funds). Raw indexes don't have annual expense ratios, whereas actual investment products (such as exchange-traded funds and mutual funds) do have expense ratios.

**Table 3.3 Indexes Included in the 40-Year Seven-Asset Portfolio (1970–2009)**

| Asset Class | Underlying Index |
| --- | --- |
| Large-cap U.S. Stock | S&P 500 Index 1970–2009 |
| Small-cap U.S. Stock | Ibbotson Small Companies Index 1970–1978<br>Russell 2000 Index 1979–2009 |
| Non–U.S. Stock | MSCI Europe, AustralAsia, Far East Index (EAFE) 1970–2009 |
| Real Estate | NAREIT Index (National Assoc. of Real Estate Investment Trusts) 1970–1977<br>Dow Jones U.S. Select REIT Index 1978–2009 |
| Commodities | S&P Goldman Sachs Commodities Index (GSCI) 1970–2009 |
| U.S. Bonds | Ibbotson Intermediate Term Govt. Bond Index 1970–1975<br>Barclays Capital Aggregate Bond Index 1976–2009 |
| Cash | 3-Month Treasury Bill 1970–2009 |

As shown in Table 3.4, a seven-asset portfolio (with annually rebalanced equal allocations of 14.29 percent to each of the seven assets) dominated the one-asset and two-asset portfolios. Over this 40-year period, the seven-asset portfolio had a 40-year average annual return of 10.5 percent and a worst-case three-year loss of −13.3 percent. By comparison, the one-asset portfolio had a 9.9 percent average annual return and a worst-case three-year loss of almost −38 percent. The two-asset portfolio, which represents the typical "balanced" mutual fund, had a 40-year average annualized return of 9.6 percent and a worst-case three-year loss of −13.4 percent.

The seven-asset portfolio delivered better performance (measured annually and over rolling three-year periods) and did so with less or comparable risk (measured three different

**Table 3.4   Risk and Performance of Portfolios over a 40-Year Period (1970–2009)**

| | One-Asset Portfolio | Two-Asset Portfolio | Seven-Asset Portfolio |
|---|---|---|---|
| | 100% Large-cap U.S. Stock (%) | 60% Large-cap U.S. Stock/40% U.S. Bonds (%) | 14.29% Equal Allocation across seven indexes (%) |
| **Risk Measures** | | | |
| Standard Deviation of Annual Returns | 18.1 | 11.9 | 10.6 |
| Worst 3-Year Cumulative Loss | −37.6 | −13.4 | −13.3 |
| Percent of Time Underwater (38 3-year rolling periods) | 18 | 8 | 5 |
| **Performance Measures** | | | |
| 40-Year Average Annual Return | 9.9 | 9.6 | 10.5 |
| Average Rolling 3-Year Return | 10.7 | 10.0 | 11.0 |

ways). When diversification is done right, it becomes a double-edged sword that cuts to your advantage both ways—better performance with less risk.

It's worth noting that moving from a one-asset portfolio to a two-asset portfolio produces meaningful risk reduction. However, to capture the real power of diversification as a performance enhancer (as well as a risk reducer), more than two asset classes are needed. In this case, seven asset classes interacted within the portfolio to produce a 40-year average annual performance "premium" of 90 basis points (there are 100 basis points in 1 percentage point). The 10.5 percent average return of the seven-asset portfolio is 90 basis points higher than the 9.6 percent return of the two-asset portfolio.

This 40-year analysis confirms what we discovered in the 10-year analysis: More diversification delivers better performance with less risk (see Figure 3.2).

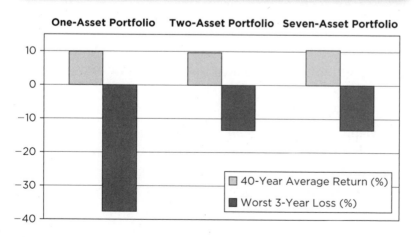

**7TWELVE**

When diversification is done right, it becomes a double-edged sword that cuts to your advantage both ways—better performance with less risk.

Figure 3.2   40-Year Period: 1970–2009

## Diversification Requires Depth *and* Breadth

As we reflect on the title of this chapter, "The More Ingredients, the Better," let's reflect on what we've learned thus far about how to diversify an investment portfolio.

First, a diversified portfolio needs to use diversified ingredients. The 7Twelve portfolio uses 12 different mutual funds (and/or exchange-traded funds) that are individually diversified—that is, each individual fund invests in hundreds of different "things" (stocks, bonds, commodities, and so on). This type of diversification represents depth. In other words, each separate component of the portfolio is a diversified basket of stuff. Investors that use mutual funds to build their portfolios usually have sufficient diversification "depth," because mutual funds are collections of hundreds or thousands of one type of specific asset (large-cap U.S. stocks, small non-U.S. stocks, and so on). Refer back to Table 1.8 to see how much "stuff" is in each of the 12 ingredients.

Second, a diversified portfolio needs to invest across many different asset classes—each of which has depth. This strategy represents diversification breadth. Most portfolios lack sufficient breadth because investors (or their advisors) assume that diversification depth is all that is needed. In fact, most mutual funds and exchange-traded funds have adequate diversification depth. For example, mutual funds that mimic the S&P 500 Index invest in 500 large-cap U.S. stocks—and that represents adequate diversification depth. Diversification breadth is achieved by building a portfolio with a wide variety of individually diversified "components" (mutual funds).

Depth is naturally achieved within each of the 12 mutual fund "components." Many investors need more breadth in their diversification. The 7Twelve portfolio represents a recipe for achieving diversification breadth.

This chapter compared the risk–reward characteristics of portfolios with various levels of diversification "breadth" and "depth." The first portfolio was a one-asset portfolio that represented a 100 percent allocation to large-cap U.S. stock (the S&P 500 Index). As shown below, this portfolio has diversification depth (500 different stocks) but no diversification breadth. As already shown, over the 10-year period and the 40-year period it exposed an investor to much higher risk (by each of three different risk measures).

**Lack of Diversification Breadth in a One-Asset Portfolio**

| Diversification Breadth | | | | | | |
|---|---|---|---|---|---|---|
| U.S. Stock | Non-U.S. Stock | Real Estate | Resources | U.S. Bonds | Non-U.S. Bonds | Cash |
| *Large Company* **Depth** | | | | | | |
| | | | | | | |
| | | | | | | |

Next, we analyzed the risk–reward characteristics of a two-asset portfolio that allocated 60 percent to large-cap U.S. stock and 40 percent to U.S. bonds. As shown below, a two-fund (or two-asset) portfolio provides only minimal diversification breadth. Of the 12 boxes, only two are filled in.

**Lack of Diversification Breadth in a Two-Asset Portfolio**

| Diversification Breadth | | | | | | |
|---|---|---|---|---|---|---|
| U.S. Stock | Non-U.S. Stock | Real Estate | Resources | U.S. Bonds | Non-U.S. Bonds | Cash |
| *Large Company* **Depth** | | | | *U.S. Aggregate Bond* **Depth** | | |
| | | | | | | |
| | | | | | | |

Compared to the one-asset portfolio, the two-asset portfolio provided improvement in risk reduction over both time periods (10 years and 40 years). Performance for the two-asset portfolio was significantly better than the one-asset portfolio over the 10-year period from 2000 to 2009. Over the 40-year period, the performance of the two-asset portfolio was actually lower than the one-asset portfolio—but provided dramatically lower risk.

Finally, we compared the 7Twelve portfolio against a one-fund and two-fund portfolio over the 10-year period from 2000 to 2009. As illustrated below, the 7Twelve portfolio achieves optimal diversification breadth. During one of the worst decades in history for investors, the 7Twelve portfolio provided a 10-year average annualized return of 7.8 percent compared to 2.6 percent for the two-fund portfolio and –1.0 percent for the one-fund portfolio.

The 7Twelve portfolio outperformed while subjecting investors to far less risk. The worst three-year cumulative percentage loss for the one-fund portfolio was nearly 38 percent and over 13 percent for the two-fund portfolio. The 7Twelve portfolio only lost 3.2 percent in its worst three-year period.

**Achievement of Diversification Breadth in the 7Twelve Portfolio**

| Diversification Breadth | | | | | | |
|---|---|---|---|---|---|---|
| U.S. Stock | Non-U.S. Stock | Real Estate | Resources | U.S. Bonds | Non-U.S. Bonds | Cash |
| Large Company *Depth* | Developed Markets *Depth* | Real Estate *Depth* | Natural Resources *Depth* | U.S. Aggregate Bond *Depth* | International Bond *Depth* | U.S. Cash *Depth* |
| Medium-sized Company *Depth* | Emerging Markets *Depth* | | Commodities *Depth* | Inflation-Protected Bond *Depth* | | |
| Small Company *Depth* | | | | | | |

Finally, if risk is measured by frequency and magnitude of losses (measured in actual account value dollars), the 7Twelve portfolio shines (see Table 3.5). Since January 1, 2000, a 100 percent allocation in large-cap U.S. stock (S&P 500 Index) has experienced losses in ending account value in four of the eight three-year rolling periods. Being underwater 50 percent of the time is not a pleasant experience for an investor. In fact, frequent losses often motivate investors to bail out of their investment at an inopportune moment, which typically makes their overall investing experience even less rewarding.

A two-fund 60/40 portfolio was a slight improvement, but over rolling three-year periods was still underwater 25 percent of the time (two out of eight rolling three-year periods). The 7Twelve portfolio was only underwater during one three-year period (2006–2008). Over that particular three-year period, a $10,000 initial investment was worth $9,676 after three years— a very small loss. Interestingly, the 7Twelve portfolio had better upside performance (larger ending account values during

**Table 3.5   Ending Account Values over Rolling 3-Year Periods (starting balance of $10,000 at the start of each 3-year period)**

| Rolling 3-Year Period | 100% U.S. Large-cap U.S. Stock ($) | 60% Large-cap U.S. Stock/40% U.S. Bond Portfolio ($) | 7Twelve Portfolio ($) |
|---|---|---|---|
| 2000–2002 | 6,248 | 8,662 | 10,438 |
| 2001–2003 | 8,867 | 10,391 | 12,423 |
| 2002–2004 | 11,136 | 11,675 | 14,861 |
| 2003–2005 | 14,876 | 13,300 | 16,802 |
| 2004–2006 | 13,442 | 12,478 | 15,255 |
| 2005–2007 | 12,765 | 12,214 | 14,415 |
| 2006–2008 | 7,706 | 9,568 | 9,676 |
| 2007–2009 | 8,406 | 10,069 | 10,482 |
| Average 3-Year Ending Account Balance | **10,431** | **11,045** | **13,044** |

the "good" three-year periods). Better downside protection and better upside performance—broadly diversified portfolios are a lovely thing.

Hopefully, this chapter has provided a compelling case for diversification depth and breadth. The grand key to the 7Twelve portfolio recipe is diversification *breadth.*

Chapter 4 delves more deeply into the performance of a portfolio that provides diversification breadth—namely, the 7Twelve portfolio.

CHAPTER 4

# GROWTH OF MONEY

As demonstrated in Chapter 3, portfolios with more diversification tend to have less risk. Portfolios with more diversification also tend to have performance that is much more stable from year to year, and stable return patterns generally produce higher average returns. This chapter takes a more in-depth look at the performance benefit produced by broad diversification.

The most common way of measuring performance is to calculate the average annual return of an investment, which is measured in percentage terms. Technically speaking, this is known as the *geometric mean*. Okay, no more geek talk.

Perhaps a more useful and intuitive way to evaluate the effectiveness of an investment portfolio is to measure how it grows money or loses money over time. Growth of money is the most pragmatic measure of an investment portfolio's performance.

This chapter compares the performance of the 7Twelve portfolio to the performance of one-fund and two-fund portfolios over a 10-year term. Observing the annual returns of each portfolio over 10 years demonstrates the importance of a diversified portfolio when the economy is up *and* when the economy is down.

## 7TWELVE

A useful and intuitive way to evaluate the effectiveness of an investment portfolio is to measure how it grows money or loses money over time.

## Why Measure Growth of Money?

A portfolio that fails to grow money over a 10-year period is an unacceptable portfolio, or at least a very unsatisfying portfolio. Let's face it—we all care about results. Like it or not, we are all "outcome-based" investors. Growth and/or protection of our invested dollars is the ultimate outcome.

As shown in Figure 4.1, the 7Twelve portfolio did a much better job growing money compared to a sole investment in U.S. large-cap stock (S&P 500 Index). The 7Twelve portfolio also outperformed a 60 percent large-cap U.S. stock and 40 percent U.S. bond portfolio over the past 10 years. The 7Twelve portfolio turned a $10,000 initial investment on January 1, 2000, into $21,212 by December 31, 2009. The ending balance in 100 percent U.S. large-cap stock (a one-fund portfolio) was $9,047, while the 60/40 portfolio ended with $12,921. Annual rebalancing was assumed.

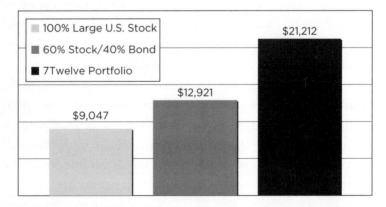

**Figure 4.1  10-Year Growth of $10,000 from January 1, 2000, to December 31, 2009**

The growth (and protection) of money is arguably the most "real-world" measure of performance. Therefore, the volatility in the growth of money is perhaps the most "real-world" measure of risk. Figure 4.2 demonstrates the month-to-month growth of a $10,000 investment into the three different portfolios (one-fund, two-fund, and 7Twelve). This graph represents the monthly growth and decline in account value, which is the way we experience portfolio risk as investors.

The two-fund 60 percent stock/40 percent bond portfolio in Figure 4.2 was rebalanced monthly back to the 60/40 allocation. The 7Twelve portfolio, with its 12 equally weighted mutual funds, was also rebalanced monthly back to an 8.33 percent allocation per fund. A later chapter will discuss rebalancing in more detail.

During the turmoil of 2000–2002, the U.S. stock market had negative returns for three straight years, as measured by the S&P 500 Index. As shown by the solid line in Figure 4.2, the 7Twelve portfolio sailed through that three-year period unscathed. Conversely, a 100 percent large-cap U.S. stock investment (a one-fund portfolio depicted by the dotted line) and a 60/40 portfolio (a two-fund portfolio depicted by the dash line) suffered significant dollar losses—meaning that the account value dipped below the initial investment of $10,000. In fact, by the end of 2002, the $10,000 initial investment in the 100 percent stock portfolio had been cut nearly in half. Investors are like airline passengers—they prefer a smooth ride.

As shown in Figure 4.2, the subsequent five-year period (2003–2007) was a period of impressive growth for the 7Twelve portfolio. Not only did the 7Twelve protect the portfolio during the downturn from 2000 to 2002, but it outperformed the other two portfolios when the markets were on the upside.

The mayhem of 2008 dramatically affected all three portfolios, but as shown in Figure 4.2, by the end of 2009 the 7Twelve portfolio had recouped most of the loss it experienced in 2008. The year 2008 was an ugly reminder that even

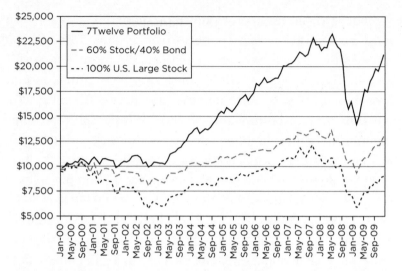

**Figure 4.2  Monthly Growth of $10,000 from January 1, 2000, to December 31, 2009**

mega-diversification is not a bullet-proof portfolio strategy. Few, if any, things in life are bullet-proof.

## Expect Ups and Downs

Despite losses in 2008, the 7Twelve portfolio has demonstrated that breadth of diversification is as important as depth of diversification—and that achieving both types of diversification produces superior risk-adjusted performance. The unusually volatile investment markets of 2008 didn't change that.

When examined over the past 10 years, the 7Twelve portfolio has provided a smoother ride for an investor as measured by:

1. Growth of money
2. Volatility in the growth of money

The annual returns for all three portfolios are shown below in Table 4.1. The returns reflect annual rebalancing (more on that in Chapter 6).

**Table 4.1  Annual Returns of Three Portfolios**

| Year | One-Fund Portfolio* 100% Large-cap U.S. Stock (%) | Two-Fund Portfolio** 60% Large-cap U.S. Stock/40% U.S. Bonds (%) | 12-Fund Portfolio 7Twelve Portfolio (%) |
|---|---|---|---|
| 2000 | −9.70 | −1.22 | 6.78 |
| 2001 | −11.86 | −3.79 | −1.58 |
| 2002 | −21.50 | −8.85 | −0.68 |
| 2003 | 28.16 | 18.49 | 27.08 |
| 2004 | 10.69 | 8.10 | 17.73 |
| 2005 | 4.86 | 3.84 | 12.30 |
| 2006 | 15.80 | 11.16 | 15.38 |
| 2007 | 5.12 | 5.81 | 11.25 |
| 2008 | −36.70 | −18.66 | −24.62 |
| 2009 | 26.32 | 17.22 | 24.99 |
| 3-Year Average Annualized Return (2007–2009) | **−5.63** | **0.30** | **1.58** |
| 5-Year Average Annualized Return (2005–2009) | **0.41** | **3.09** | **6.31** |
| 10-Year Average Annualized Return (2000–2009) | **−1.00** | **2.60** | **7.81** |
| 10-Year Standard Deviation of Annual Returns (2000–2009) | **20.90** | **11.63** | **15.11** |
| 10-Year Growth of $10,000 | **$9,047** | **$12,921** | **$21,212** |

*Using SPY.
**Using 60% SPY/40% LAG.
*Note*: Annual rebalancing assumed for Two-Fund Portfolio and 12-Fund Portfolio.

The annual returns of the individual mutual funds (in this case, ETFs) in the 7Twelve portfolio are shown in Table 4.2. The past decade (2000–2009) was the second worst decade ever for investors as measured by the 10-year return of the S&P 500 Index. The 10-year period from 2000 to 2009 is a perfect test case for evaluating the benefits of building a diversified portfolio.

**Table 4.2 Annual Returns 7Twelve Portfolio and Individual Ingredients from 2000 to 2009**

| Year | Large-cap U.S. Stock (%) | Mid U.S. Stock (%) | Small-cap U.S. Stock (%) | Non-U.S. Stock (%) | Emerging Stock (%) | Real Estate (%) | Resources (%) | Commodities (%) | U.S. Bonds (%) | TIPS (%) | International Bonds (%) | Cash (%) | 7Twelve Portfolio (%) |
|---|---|---|---|---|---|---|---|---|---|---|---|---|---|
| 2000 | -9.70 | 17.38 | 21.88 | -14.46 | -27.45 | 26.46 | 15.24 | 24.43 | 11.49 | 12.95 | -3.13 | 6.29 | **6.78** |
| 2001 | -11.86 | -0.90 | 13.70 | -21.71 | -2.73 | 12.45 | -16.00 | -8.68 | 8.31 | 7.68 | -3.41 | 4.16 | **-1.58** |
| 2002 | -21.50 | -14.51 | -14.20 | -15.43 | -7.29 | 3.85 | -13.49 | 24.56 | 10.12 | 16.33 | 21.80 | 1.65 | **-0.68** |
| 2003 | 28.16 | 35.26 | 37.19 | 57.88 | 39.71 | 35.77 | 33.37 | 25.84 | 3.98 | 8.18 | 18.78 | 0.90 | **27.08** |
| 2004 | 10.69 | 15.89 | 23.55 | 26.31 | 18.94 | 30.87 | 24.38 | 37.15 | 4.21 | 8.29 | 11.41 | 1.11 | **17.73** |
| 2005 | 4.86 | 12.51 | 6.18 | 32.25 | 13.35 | 11.99 | 35.96 | 30.87 | 2.31 | 2.52 | -8.18 | 3.01 | **12.30** |
| 2006 | 15.80 | 9.96 | 19.38 | 29.20 | 25.79 | 35.05 | 16.40 | 16.02 | 4.21 | 0.29 | 7.55 | 4.88 | **15.38** |
| 2007 | 5.12 | 7.20 | -6.94 | 37.32 | 9.94 | -16.51 | 33.45 | 31.50 | 6.84 | 11.93 | 10.06 | 5.14 | **11.25** |
| 2008 | -36.70 | -36.39 | -32.19 | -52.46 | -41.01 | -36.91 | -42.88 | -31.73 | 8.41 | -0.53 | 4.22 | 2.77 | **-24.62** |
| 2009 | 26.32 | 37.52 | 30.93 | 76.32 | 26.88 | 30.11 | 37.11 | 16.18 | 3.57 | 8.96 | 5.43 | 0.53 | **24.99** |
| 10-Year Average Annualized Return | **-1.00** | **6.10** | **7.76** | **1.00** | **9.88** | **10.52** | **8.67** | **14.49** | **6.30** | **7.53** | **6.06** | **3.03** | **7.81** |
| 10-Year Standard Deviation of Annual Returns | **20.90** | **21.97** | **21.78** | **25.87** | **39.23** | **24.14** | **27.38** | **21.17** | **3.12** | **5.49** | **9.64** | **2.01** | **15.11** |
| 10-Year Growth of $10,000 | **$9,047** | **$18,083** | **$21,106** | **$11,041** | **$25,657** | **$27,198** | **$22,975** | **$38,683** | **$18,430** | **$20,674** | **$18,011** | **$13,474** | **$21,212** |

*Note:* Annual returns in this table reflect the performance of actual ETFs that comprise the 7Twelve "Passive" portfolio.

The far-right column in Table 4.2 shows the year-to-year returns of the equally weighted 7Twelve portfolio with annual rebalancing. The 7Twelve portfolio had a positive return of 6.78 percent in 2000, which was a rough year for U.S. large-cap stock (–9.7 percent) and non–U.S. stock (–14.5 percent for developed non-U.S. countries and –27.5 percent for emerging non–U.S. stock). The power of diversification comes from spreading investment dollars across many different asset classes: diversification breadth. In the year 2000, diversification *breadth* worked just as designed.

In 2001, the 7Twelve portfolio had a small loss of 1.58 percent. By comparison, large-cap U.S. stock lost nearly 12 percent, developed non–U.S. stock lost 21.7 percent, emerging non-U.S. stock lost nearly 3 percent, natural resources lost 16 percent, and commodities lost nearly 9 percent. Once again, we see the benefit of diversification. Small-cap U.S. stock with a value tilt (more on what that means in Chapter 9) had a positive return of 13.7 percent, real estate was up over 12 percent, U.S. bonds had a positive return of 8.3 percent, inflation protected bonds (TIPS) were up almost 7.7 percent, and cash had a positive return of over 4 percent. By spreading risk, the 7Twelve portfolio avoided the large losses experienced by several of the individual funds in the 7Twelve portfolio.

The year 2002 is another good example of how diversification lowers portfolio risk. In 2002, large-cap U.S. stock lost 21.5 percent, midcap U.S. stock lost 14.5 percent, and small-cap U.S. stock with a value tilt lost 14.2 percent. Developed non–U.S. stock lost 15.4 percent and emerging non–U.S. stock lost 7.3 percent. Natural resources lost 13.5 percent. Half of the 12 funds had nasty negative returns. But the other half had positive returns. Real estate was up nearly 4 percent, commodities were up 24.6 percent, U.S. bonds had a 10.1 percent return, TIPS were up 16.3 percent, non–U.S. bonds had a positive return of nearly 22 percent, and cash was up nearly 1.7 percent. Thus, in sum, 2002 was a great year for the 7Twelve portfolio in comparison to the losses experienced in the U.S. and non–U.S. stock markets.

Does a broadly diversified portfolio, such as the 7Twelve portfolio, lag behind when stock and bond markets are having good years? No. For example, in 2003, the S&P 500 Index was up over 28 percent. The 7Twelve portfolio had a return of 27.1 percent. In 2004, the S&P 500 was up 10.7 percent and the 7Twelve portfolio had a return of 17.7 percent. In 2006, the S&P 500 had a 15.8 percent return while the 7Twelve portfolio produced a one-year gain of 15.4 percent.

In summary, the upside performance of the diversified 7Twelve portfolio has been comparable or better than the S&P 500 Index in good years, but with far better downside protection during the bad years.

Speaking of downside protection, even the 7Twelve portfolio took a hit in 2008, as it lost 24.6 percent. As shown in Table 4.2, large-cap U.S. stock (as measured by SPY, an ETF that attempts to mimic the S&P 500 Index) lost 36.7 percent. Midcap U.S. stock lost 36.4 percent in 2008, developed non–U.S. stock lost 41.01 percent, and emerging non–U.S. stock lost 52.46 percent.

What hurt the 7Twelve portfolio in 2008 were the simultaneous losses in real estate and commodities—in conjunction with the losses in U.S. and non–U.S. stock markets. Historically speaking, real estate and commodities tend to behave differently than U.S. and non–U.S. stock. When stock is down, real estate and commodities are usually up. That didn't happen in 2008. However, it is worth noting that as of September 30, 2008, both the real estate fund and the commodities fund had positive year-to-date returns despite large losses in all five stock funds (U.S. large-cap, U.S. midcap, U.S. small-cap, developed non–U.S., and emerging non–U.S.). The meltdown of 2008 really occurred during October and November 2008 because that's when the "diversifying" assets (real estate, commodities, and even TIPS) got hammered.

However, even in 2008, three of the 12 mutual funds in the 7Twelve portfolio had positive returns: U.S. bonds, non–U.S. bonds, and cash. This is a perfect example of diversification providing a safe haven during one of the worst investing storms in history. If an investor needed to make a withdrawal during 2008, he or she could have done so from those three funds in the 7Twelve portfolio without having to draw money from a fund that was battered.

The 7Twelve is a fully diversified portfolio that has consistently produced better performance with less risk than the typical 60/40 balanced fund or S&P 500 Index fund. As a fully diversified portfolio, the 7Twelve portfolio represents the ideal nucleus of virtually any portfolio.

When building a portfolio, start with the 7Twelve recipe and then mix in whatever other assets will help you meet your needs and objectives. For example, if you want to emphasize growth in your portfolio, you might allocate half of your investment to the 7Twelve portfolio and the other half to several mutual funds that are specifically growth oriented. Conversely, if you need to emphasize capital preservation, you might allocate half of your investment to the 7Twelve and the other half to fixed income funds or an annuity product.

In summary, every portfolio should be diversified at its core—and that's what the 7Twelve is: a broadly diversified portfolio. The 7Twelve portfolio can be the diversified core of

### 7TWELVE

When building a portfolio, start with the 7Twelve recipe and then mix in whatever other assets will help you meet your needs and objectives.

any portfolio *or* it can be your entire portfolio. Like any good recipe, the 7Twelve portfolio is flexible.

In Chapter 5 we'll examine the issue of correlation between the ingredients in a portfolio. Hint: the lower the correlation, the better.

# COMBINING INGREDIENTS
# THAT ZIG *AND* ZAG

A well-designed portfolio will combine investment assets that have different attributes. The core idea here is expressed in the classic advice "Don't put all your eggs in one basket." If you drop the basket, you're toast. (Technically you would be egged, but you get the point.)

By diversifying across various unrelated investment assets, your portfolio should be less susceptible to large losses. And if we can avoid or minimize large losses, our overall investment experience should be better.

Ever wondered why stocks and bonds are combined in the classic 60/40 portfolio? It's because stocks and bonds behave differently. Their performance "attributes" are different. Bonds tend to have positive returns, while stock performance is more erratic with greater upside potential and downside risk than bonds. One way of measuring differences between investment assets is by calculating the correlation between them. Very simply, if two different investments move in the same direction at the same time, they have high correlation. If they move in opposite directions most of the time, they have low correlation.

In this chapter, we'll discuss why building a portfolio with ingredients that have low correlation to each other is desirable.

## Getting Close to Zero

A correlation of 1.00 indicates complete positive symmetry between two things. When one goes up, the other goes up; when one goes down, the other goes down. For example, there is high correlation between time spent practicing the piano and the quality of piano performance. More practice is highly correlated to better performance. As one goes up, the other goes up.

Alternatively, a correlation of −1.00 indicates perfect negative symmetry. When one thing goes down, the other always goes up (and vice versa). Being critical of others has a negative correlation with quality of friendship. As critical comments increase, quality of friendship decreases.

A correlation of zero between two things indicates that the movement of the two things is unrelated—or in other words, they have a random correlation. When building portfolios, combining investment assets that have low correlation to each other is the goal. Said differently, we want the average correlation among all the portfolio components to be close to zero. This is difficult to achieve, but it represents the ideal goal.

There are many real-life examples of the importance of low correlation among the components of a system. We've already considered a salsa analogy. Another example is a basketball team that needs players with different attributes and talents— it needs to be a diversified team. Building a basketball team with five point guards is not a great idea, as much as we value

**7TWELVE**

When building your portfolio, combining assets that have low correlation to each other is the goal.

| 7TWELVE |
|---|
| Low correlation between the various parts of any system equals diversification. This is particularly important when building investment portfolios. |

point guards. A center is needed, as well as several forwards. Because they have different attributes and talents, the correlation between point guards and power forwards is low—and low correlation is what we're after. Low correlation between the various parts of any system equals diversification. This is particularly important when building investment portfolios.

## Finding Assets That Play Nicely Together

The 7Twelve portfolio is diversified because it combines investment assets that are different from each other. The differences are valuable because if one investment is having a bad year, the portfolio will rely on (and benefit from) other assets that are having a good year. If you build a portfolio with several mutual funds that are all similar to each other, they stand a higher chance of all having a bad year at the same time—and that's a bad feeling. Sort of like getting egged.

Let me illustrate with two simple three-asset portfolios. All examples in this section use data from the 40-year period from 1970 to 2009. Portfolio A combines large-cap U.S. stock, small-cap U.S. stock, and non–U.S. stock. Portfolio B combines large-cap U.S. stock, U.S. bonds, and commodities (see Table 5.1). Portfolio A represents a high-correlation portfolio, while Portfolio B is a low-correlation portfolio.

The weakness of Portfolio A is that each of the three assets is too highly correlated. The 40-year correlation between large-cap U.S. stock and small-cap U.S. stock is 0.78, and the correlation between large-cap U.S. stock and non–U.S. stock

**Table 5.1  Performance Comparison of a High-Correlation Portfolio to a Low-Correlation Portfolio (1970–2009)**

|  | Portfolio A (high) | Portfolio B (low) |
| --- | --- | --- |
| Ingredients (weighted equally) | Large-cap U.S. stock<br>Small-cap U.S. stock<br>Non–U.S. stock | Large-cap U.S. stock<br>U.S. bonds<br>Commodities |
| Average Correlation among Ingredients | 0.66 | 0.02 |
| 40-Year Standard Deviation of Annual Returns | 18.6% | 10.4% |
| Worst 3-Year Cumulative Loss | −34.1% | −13.5% |
| Growth of $10,000 | $529,185 | $542,447 |
| 40-Year Average Annual Return | 10.4% | 10.5% |

is 0.66—both very high correlations. The correlation between small-cap U.S. stock and non–U.S. stock has been 0.54 over the past 40 years—also quite high. All three assets tend to move up or down at the same time, which is not the goal of a diversified portfolio. The average correlation in Portfolio A is .66.

Portfolio B combines large-cap U.S. stock, bonds, and commodities—each of which has low correlation to each other. The 40-year correlation between large-cap U.S. stock and bonds has been 0.26. The correlation between large-cap U.S. stock and commodities has been –0.07, and the correlation between bonds and commodities has been –0.14. The average correlation among the three ingredients in Portfolio B is 0.02.

The return patterns of the three assets in Portfolio A are too similar. By comparison, the return patterns of the assets in Portfolio B are dissimilar—which is how portfolio diversification is achieved.

The 40-year average annual return for Portfolio B was slightly higher than Portfolio A (10.5 percent vs. 10.4 percent).

The ultimate measure of success in a portfolio is performance, whether measured as a percentage return or the growth of $10,000. By both measures, the low-correlation portfolio was superior. Interestingly, Portfolio B outperformed Portfolio A even though the average return of its three individual ingredients was actually lower than the average return of the three separate ingredients in Portfolio A (9.4 percent in Portfolio B vs. 10.0 percent in Portfolio A).

This perfectly illustrates the "portfolio effect." When combined in a portfolio, low-correlation ingredients create an outcome that exceeds the sum of their parts. This is observed in so many ways. When a barbershop quartet hits a chord just right, it creates an "overtone"—a fifth note that represents a sound that was not created by an individual but through the interactive harmony of the group. It is a synergistic result where the whole is greater than the sum of the parts. Combining ingredients that have high correlation with each other is much less likely to produce this desirable "portfolio effect."

The "portfolio effect" phenomenon is similar to what happened to the U.S. men's Olympic basketball team in 2004—a team of individual superstars that failed to win the gold medal. The moral of this story is very simple: It's a team game. Likewise, in a portfolio, it's not about simply combining a bunch of superstar mutual funds. A thoughtfully designed portfolio (team) combines a variety of funds (athletes) that have low correlation with each other (play well together).

Reducing risk in a portfolio is also vitally important. We observe that the standard deviation of return in Portfolio A was nearly two times higher than Portfolio B. Even more dramatic is the difference in the worst three-year cumulative percentage return. Portfolio A lost 34.1 percent in its worst three-year period, while Portfolio B only lost 13.5 percent in its worst three-year period. The high correlation portfolio was far more risky than the low correlation portfolio.

It's important to remember that the portfolio effect is not so much a performance enhancer (though it can be), but rather a powerful risk reducer.

## Don't Forget Broad Diversification

Let's now examine various portfolios, moving from the simple three-asset portfolios demonstrated in Table 5.1 to progressively more diversified portfolios (see Table 5.2). The analysis in Table 5.2 uses the seven core asset categories (indexes) that you're already familiar with: large-cap U.S. stock, small-cap U.S. stock, non–U.S. stock, real estate, commodities, bonds, and cash. I'll demonstrate the performance attributes as we move from a one-asset portfolio to a seven-asset portfolio. The time frame of the analysis is the 40-year period from 1970 to 2009. The starting point is a one-asset portfolio consisting entirely of large-cap U.S. stock (100 percent S&P 500 Index). Because this is a one-asset portfolio, the overall portfolio correlation is 1.00 or 100 percent. The correlation of one asset to itself is, by definition, 1.00 or 100 percent. The 40-year average annualized return of the one-asset portfolio was 9.9 percent, which turned an initial investment of $10,000 in 1970 into over $431,000 by the end of 2009.

The one-asset portfolio has a serious drawback—it had a three-year period in which it lost of cumulative total of 37.6 percent. Losses of that magnitude can be unsettling to even the most intrepid investor. In fact, large losses will often lead to erratic portfolio adjustments by panicking investors. The goal, therefore, of a well-diversified low-correlation portfolio is to produce equity-like returns with bond-like risk. Steady portfolio performance leads to better outcomes because investors are less likely to bail out at the wrong time.

The second portfolio is a two-asset portfolio that blends large-cap U.S. stock and small-cap U.S. stock in equal portions. While this may seem to create diversification, it doesn't. Notice that the correlation between large-cap U.S. stock and

**Table 5.2   Approaching Low Correlation by Increasing Diversification (1970–2009)**

| Portfolio Ingredients (weighted equally) | 40-Year Annualized Return (%) | 40-year Growth of $10,000 ($) | Worst 3-Year Cumulative Loss (%) | Average Portfolio Correlation |
|---|---|---|---|---|
| Large-cap U.S. Stock | 9.9 | 431,842 | −37.6 | 1.00 |
| Large-cap U.S. Stock Small-cap U.S. Stock | 10.5 | 537,327 | −33.8 | 0.78 |
| Large-cap U.S. Stock Small-cap U.S. Stock Non–U.S. Stock | 10.4 | 529,185 | −34.1 | 0.66 |
| Large-cap U.S. Stock Small-cap U.S. Stock Non–U.S. Stock Bonds | 10.3 | 497,556 | −20.0 | 0.39 |
| Large-cap U.S. Stock Small-cap U.S. Stock Non–U.S. Stock Bonds Cash | 9.6 | 387,508 | −14.2 | 0.27 |
| Large-cap U.S. Stock Small-cap U.S. Stock Non–U.S. Stock Bonds Cash Real Estate | 10.0 | 448,445 | −12.1 | 0.30 |
| Large-cap U.S. Stock Small-cap U.S. Stock Non–U.S. Stock Bonds Cash Real Estate Commodities | 10.5 | 532,991 | −13.3 | 0.20 |
| Traditional Balanced Portfolio: 60% Large-cap U.S. Stock/40% U.S. Bonds | 9.6 | 397,729 | −13.4 | 0.26 |

small-cap U.S. stock is 0.78, which is a very high correlation. The behavior of the two (that is, the pattern of returns) is similar 78 percent of the time. Said differently, if large-cap U.S. stock has a positive return there is a 78 percent chance that small-cap U.S. stock will also have a positive return. High correlation works against diversification.

The 40-year return of the two-asset portfolio was 10.5 percent, which produced an ending account balance that was about $106,000 higher than the one-asset portfolio. However, the worst three-year cumulative percentage loss of the two-asset portfolio was nearly as high as the one-asset portfolio (–33.8% vs. −37.6%). This is precisely because these two assets (large-cap U.S. stock and small-cap U.S. stock) are highly correlated. They tend to zig and zag at the same time. We need a portfolio that includes components (mutual funds or exchange traded funds) that zig and zag at different times.

Next, we add non–U.S. stock to the portfolio with each asset having a 33.33 percent allocation. The average correlation among the three portfolio components declines slightly to 0.66 while the average return dips slightly to 10.4 percent. Sadly, the worst three-year cumulative loss actually increased slightly to –34.1 percent. Despite adding three "different" ingredients together, we are not seeing a beneficial reduction in downside risk because these three ingredients are too similar in their performance patterns.

Our first glimpse of a "low-correlation" effect occurs when we add bonds into the portfolio. Now we have a four-asset portfolio with a 25 percent allocation to each component. The

## 7TWELVE

Build a portfolio that includes components (mutual funds or exchange-traded funds) that have performance that zigs and zags at different times.

average correlation in the portfolio drops dramatically to 0.39 because of the low correlation that bonds have to each of the three equity ingredients. The 40-year annualized return declines only slightly to 10.3 percent while the worst three-year cumulative return improves from –34.1 percent to –20.0 percent. Now we are seeing what low correlation can do to a portfolio: maintain strong performance while reducing downside risk.

Next, we add cash to the portfolio. This five-asset portfolio gives a 20 percent allocation to each of the five ingredients. Inasmuch as cash also has low correlation to all three stock ingredients, the average portfolio correlation drops to an even lower level of 0.27. Adding cash also produces a reduction in the downside risk of the portfolio. The worst three-year return improved to –14.2 percent. The "price" of adding cash was a reduction in the average annual return of the portfolio from 10.3 percent to 9.6 percent. However, compared to the 100 percent large-cap U.S. stock portfolio, the ending account balance was only $44,334 lower while the downside risk was lowered by over 60 percent from –37.6 percent to –14.2 percent. That is a good trade-off.

The next two portfolio ingredients reveal the stuff low-correlation portfolios are made of. When real estate is added to the mix, the average portfolio correlation ticks up slightly to 0.30 but the return jumps up to 10.0 percent and the worst three-year return improves to –12.1 percent. Unlike small-cap U.S. stock and non–U.S. stock, real estate does not always have negative returns when large-cap U.S. stock does. That's the key to low correlation. Real estate particularly helped out during the rough years of 2000–2002. In each of those years, real estate had a positive return while large-cap U.S. stock suffered three consecutive negative returns.

Finally, adding commodities to the portfolio (now each of the seven assets has a 14.29 percent allocation) produces spectacular results. The overall portfolio correlation declines to 0.20 because the commodities fund has very low correlation to every other ingredient in the portfolio. The average annual return of the seven-asset portfolio increased to 10.5 percent, which produced an ending account value that was approximately $100,000 greater than a one-asset portfolio consisting entirely of U.S. large-cap stock. Equally important is the fact that the downside risk improved dramatically. The worst three-year cumulative return for the seven-asset portfolio was −13.3 percent, or about one-third the risk of a 100 percent investment in the S&P 500 Index.

At the bottom of Table 5.2 is the classic 60/40 balanced portfolio. It has a 60 percent allocation to large-cap U.S. stock and a 40 percent allocation to U.S. bonds. For decades, this model has been the mainstay of what is termed a "balanced" portfolio. As you can see, the correlation between stocks and bonds is impressively low at 0.26.

This two-asset portfolio meets the criterion of a low-correlation portfolio. However, it does not achieve the equally important criterion of broad diversification. Between 1970 and 2009, the two-asset 60/40 portfolio produced a 40-year average annualized return of 9.6 percent, far below the 10.5 percent return of the broadly diversified seven-asset portfolio. This return difference amounted to about $135,000 larger account balance in the seven-asset portfolio. Diversification does have benefits!

The seven-asset portfolio over the 40-year period from 1970 to 2009 has demonstrated, yet again, the importance of broad diversification when building an investment portfolio. In fact, it was this seven-asset portfolio that inspired the creation of the 7Twelve portfolio.

## 7TWELVE

It was the seven-asset portfolio that inspired the creation of the 7Twelve portfolio.

One of the distinctive advantages of a multi-asset portfolio (using seven different investments in this case) is a reduction in the frequency of losses. Over this 40-year period, the seven-asset portfolio had only five years with a negative return. By comparison, large-cap U.S. stock (S&P 500 Index) suffered nine negative annual returns and the two-asset 60/40 portfolio suffered annual losses in seven years. Not only were losses less frequent in the seven-asset portfolio, they were also smaller on average.

The underlying indexes in the seven-asset portfolio from Table 5.2 were previously listed in Chapter 3 (see Table 3.3). Recall that the seven-asset portfolio in Table 3.3 is the precursor to the 7Twelve portfolio, which includes 12 different ingredients.

The 7Twelve portfolio contains several ingredients that don't have a performance history back to 1970. However, the seven-asset portfolio represents the essence of the 7Twelve portfolio and verifies the long-term benefits of building a portfolio that has diversification breadth because it assembles ingredients that have low correlation to each other.

Based on the performance of the seven-asset portfolio over the past 40 years, we gain insight into the anticipated relative performance of a diversified portfolio compared to investing in individual assets or a simple two-asset portfolio. Simply put, a broadly diversified portfolio provides better performance with less risk. We have compelling reasons to diversify by building portfolios that have low correlation among the various ingredients.

## Quantifying Correlation

Correlation can be measured *and* quantified. Shown in Table 5.3 are the correlations between each of the seven core assets.

The similarity in the year-to-year performance of large-cap U.S. stock, small-cap U.S. stock, and non–U.S. stock is quantified in Table 5.3. We observe that the correlation

**Table 5.3  Forty-Year Correlation among Ingredients of the Seven-Asset Portfolio**

|  | Large-cap U.S. Stock | Small-cap U.S. Stock | Non–U.S. Stock | U.S. Bonds | U.S. Cash | Real Estate |
|---|---|---|---|---|---|---|
| Small-cap U.S. Stock | 0.78 |  |  |  |  |  |
| Non–U.S. Stock | 0.66 | 0.54 |  |  |  |  |
| U.S. Bonds | 0.26 | 0.12 | −0.01 |  |  |  |
| Cash | 0.10 | 0.06 | −0.05 | 0.25 |  |  |
| Real Estate | 0.51 | 0.75 | 0.38 | 0.06 | 0.10 |  |
| Commodities | −0.07 | −0.15 | 0.03 | −0.14 | 0.09 | −0.04 |

between large-cap U.S. stock, small-cap U.S. stock, and non–U.S. stock tends to be very high (0.78 between large-cap and small-cap U.S. stock, 0.66 between large-cap U.S. and non–U.S. stock, and 0.54 between small-cap U.S. and non–U.S. stock).

Commodities, on the other hand, had a correlation of –0.07 with large-cap U.S. stock. Recall that a correlation of zero indicates no discernable connection in the behavior of the two things being compared. Thus, a correlation of –0.07 (being so close to zero) reveals that the annual return pattern of commodities has a nearly random connection to the annual return pattern of large-cap U.S. stock.

Because the correlation has a negative sign, we know that there is a slightly negative correlation between the two. That is, when large-cap U.S. stock has a positive return, there is a slightly larger than zero probability that commodities will have a negative return.

Conversely, the correlation between large-cap U.S. stock and small-cap U.S. stock is 0.78. This is a high correlation and indicates that these two assets move in the same direction 78 percent of the time.

You might be thinking that because these two assets are so highly correlated, why are both included in the portfolio? That's a fair question. It's tough to pull small-cap U.S. stock out of the portfolio because it has demonstrated great performance potential over time. Because of performance considerations, we sometimes allow certain highly correlated portfolio ingredients to coexist. Sort of like having 1 percent milk and 2 percent milk in the fridge.

The correlation information in Table 5.3 and the performance results in Table 5.2 clearly show that commodities and real estate are excellent portfolio "diversifiers" because of their low correlation to other typical portfolio ingredients such as large-cap U.S. stock, small-cap U.S. stock, non–U.S. stock, bonds, and cash. Nevertheless, commodities and real estate are viewed as "alternatives," which is a cloaked way of saying "scary assets."

The contention that commodities and real estate are dramatically more risky is untrue. Let's let actual performance data tell the real story. Three risk measures and two performance measures that were introduced in Chapter 3 are provided in Table 5.4 for the five equity (and equity-like) assets: large-cap U.S. stock, small-cap U.S. stock, non–U.S. stock, real estate, and commodities. The time frame is the 40-year period from 1970 to 2009.

If standard deviation is used as the measure of risk, real estate has lower risk than U.S. small-cap stock and non–U.S. stock. Commodities has only slightly higher risk than U.S. small-cap stock and non–U.S. stock.

If worst three-year cumulative percent return is used as the measure of risk, real estate is the least risky of the five assets, and commodities is less risky than small-cap U.S. stock and non–U.S. stock and only slightly more risky than large-cap U.S. stock.

**Table 5.4   Actual Risk of Equity Asset Classes during the 40-Year Period from 1970 to 2009**

| | Measure of Risk | | | Measure of Performance | |
|---|---|---|---|---|---|
| | Standard Deviation of Annual Returns (%) | Worst 3-Year Cumulative Return (%) | Percent of Time "Underwater" after 3 years | 40-Year Average Annual Return (%) | Average Rolling 3-Year Return (%) |
| Large-cap U.S. Stock | 18.1 | −37.6 | 18.4 | 9.9 | 10.7 |
| Small-cap U.S. Stock | 22.5 | −42.2 | 15.8 | 10.6 | 12.1 |
| Non–U.S. Stock | 23.0 | −43.3 | 23.7 | 9.5 | 10.8 |
| Real Estate | 20.0 | −35.6 | 18.4 | 11.0 | 12.3 |
| Commodities | 25.2 | −39.7 | 23.7 | 10.0 | 11.4 |

Finally, commodities and non–U.S. stock were both underwater 23.7 percent of the time (measured over the 38 rolling three-year periods between 1970 and 2009). Very few investors would reject the idea of adding international stocks to their portfolio, but they might bristle at the idea of adding commodities. Based on the three measures of risk in Table 5.4, commodities as a portfolio ingredient is comparable to small-cap U.S. stock and non–U.S. stock—but because commodities has much lower correlation to large-cap U.S. stock it is actually a better overall addition to a portfolio than small-cap U.S. stock or non–U.S. stock (if you had to choose one over the other).

The performance of commodities and real estate has been impressive over the past 40 years. Real estate, by itself, produced an average annual return of 11.0 percent, the best return of the five asset classes in Table 5.4. With a 40-year annualized return of 10.0 percent, commodities had a better return than large-cap U.S. stock and non–U.S. stock.

## Combining Ingredients That Zig *and* Zag

**Table 5.5  Best Portfolio Partners (1970 to 2009)**

| Asset Combinations (weighted equally) | 40-Year Average Annual Return (%) | Worst 3-Year Cumulative Return (%) | 40-Year Correlation |
|---|---|---|---|
| Large-cap U.S. Stock & Small-cap U.S. Stock | 10.5 | −33.8 | 0.78 |
| Large-cap U.S. Stock & Non–U.S. Stock | 10.0 | −40.4 | 0.66 |
| Large-cap U.S. Stock & Real Estate | 10.9 | −26.8 | 0.51 |
| Large-cap U.S. Stock & Commodities | 11.1 | −30.4 | −0.07 |

The average three-year return (the average of 38 rolling three-year periods) for real estate and commodities was impressive, with real estate at 12.3 percent and commodities at 11.4 percent, both higher than large-cap U.S. stock and non–U.S. stock.

As reported in Table 5.5, when real estate or commodities are added to large-cap U.S. stock (in a 50/50 allocation), good things happen. Even though small-cap U.S. stock by itself had a higher 40-year return than commodities by itself, a portfolio that combined large-cap U.S. stock and commodities (in a 50/50 ratio) had a 40-year average annual return of 11.1 percent compared to 10.5 percent if large-cap and small-cap U.S. stock were combined. In addition, the worst three-year cumulative percent return was lower if using commodities in lieu of small-cap U.S. stock.

Because of low correlation to large-cap U.S. stock, commodities or real estate are better portfolio "diversifiers" than small-cap U.S. stock or non–U.S. stock. Said differently, commodities or real estate enhance the performance of large-cap U.S. stock more than small-cap U.S. stock or non–U.S. stock.

Some people refer to commodities and real estate as *alternative* assets. I think of them as *critical* assets. Without them, as shown in Tables 5.2 and 5.5, a portfolio has lower return and higher risk. Imagine that, adding commodities and real estate can actually lower the overall risk of a portfolio. Must be a salsa thing.

The next chapter unveils one of the grand secrets of investing: systematic rebalancing. Think of it as *stirring* the portfolio. We don't want to stir too much or too little.

CHAPTER

# STIRRING THE MIX

*R*ebalancing is the systematic process of reallocating the assets within a portfolio to keep each asset's share of the portfolio in line with predetermined percentages. In simpler terms, it's how we keep the portfolio from getting "out of balance." Rebalancing assures that as time goes by our salsa recipe doesn't end up with too many onions or too little cilantro.

As mentioned in Chapter 3, monitoring and tweaking your investment portfolio on a daily basis is like checking the daily growth of a newly planted oak tree. It's just not necessary, and frankly, who has time for that? In this chapter, we'll talk about the methods for rebalancing a portfolio but also how often it should be done to produce the best returns.

The objective of portfolio rebalancing is to keep each asset's share of the portfolio in line with predetermined allocations. For example, because the 7Twelve portfolio utilizes 12 different mutual funds and the goal is for each fund to represent 8.33 percent of the total portfolio value, the portfolio will need to be rebalanced periodically to maintain the equal weighting. This is required because each fund will not likely have the same return each year.

After one year (or whatever rebalancing time frame is selected) the best performing fund will represent more than

8.33 percent of the portfolio while the worst performing fund will hold less than 8.33 percent of the portfolio. The process of rebalancing will require that a certain number of shares of the best performing funds be sold and the proceeds be used to purchase shares of the worst performing funds.

I should mention that tax efficiency within the 7Twelve portfolio can be improved if new cash flows into the portfolio (that is, additional money being invested into the 7Twelve portfolio) are used to accomplish the needed rebalance. Done correctly, the rebalancing process will equalize the account value among all 12 funds at the end of each year or beginning of each year (if rebalancing annually).

This all sounds fine and dandy, but does rebalancing improve portfolio performance? Yes. Let's look at the data.

## Rebalancing versus Buy-and-Hold

Some investors prefer to rebalance their portfolios monthly, quarterly, or annually; and some investors may choose to not rebalance their portfolio at all. This is referred to as a "buy-and-hold" strategy.

The analysis of rebalancing in this present study will use the seven-asset portfolio over the same 40-year period that we've been working with in prior chapters. The impact of rebalancing was examined by investing a total of $10,000 in the seven-asset portfolio on January 1, 1970. Each asset received 1/7th of the total investment, or $1,428.

A buy-and-hold portfolio that did not employ year-end rebalancing was also simulated. Each of the seven assets received a $1,428 initial investment (for a total portfolio investment of $10,000) at the start of 1970. No additional investments were made into any of the assets, nor were any of the seven assets rebalanced during the 40-year period. The results of both portfolios are displayed in Table 6.1. The ending balances for *each*

**Table 6.1  Ending Balances of an Annually Rebalanced Portfolio versus Buy-and-Hold Portfolio**

| | Starting Balance: 1970 ($) | Large-cap U.S. Equity ($) | Small-cap U.S. Equity ($) | Non–U.S. Equity ($) | U.S. Bonds ($) | Cash ($) | Real Estate ($) | Commodities ($) | Ending Balance in 2009 ($) |
|---|---|---|---|---|---|---|---|---|---|
| Annually Rebalanced | 10,000 | 80,871 | 81,325 | 84,273 | 67,742 | 64,052 | 82,150 | 72,577 | 532,991 |
| Buy-and-Hold | 10,000 | 61,692 | 81,539 | 53,655 | 35,061 | 14,772 | 94,156 | 64,822 | 405,696 |

*separate portfolio ingredient* represent the 40-year growth of an initial starting amount of $1,428 (before the final rebalance at the end of the fortieth year). The ending total portfolio balance (in the far right-hand column) represents the 40-year growth from an initial total starting value of $10,000 (or the sum of the $1,428 in each of the seven assets).

The ending account value of the annually rebalanced portfolio was more than $125,000 larger than the ending account balance in the buy-and-hold portfolio (see Figure 6.1).

Perhaps more significant is the massive difference in the ending account balances in bonds and cash. The annually rebalanced portfolio had a final account balance of over $67,000 in bonds, whereas the buy-and-hold portfolio had an ending balance of just over $35,000 in bonds. The final balances in cash were even more dramatic. An initial investment of $1,428 grew to over $64,000 in the rebalanced portfolio, but to just under $15,000 in the buy-and-hold portfolio. Over long

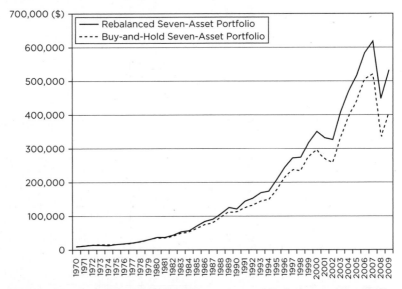

**Figure 6.1   Growth of $10,000 in an Annual Rebalanced Portfolio versus a Buy-and-Hold Portfolio**

## 7TWELVE

Over long time periods, assets that generate lower returns, such as bonds and cash, will be unable to produce account balances that keep pace with higher-returning equity-based assets unless they are rebalanced periodically.

time periods, assets that generate lower returns, such as bonds and cash, will be unable to produce account balances that keep pace with higher-returning equity-based assets—unless they are rebalanced periodically.

Why does this matter? Three words: unexpected liquidity needs. That is, an unexpected need forces us to withdraw money from our portfolio. Maintaining several assets that provide immediate liquidity within a multi-asset portfolio is vitally important. The equity carnage during 2008 is ample evidence.

Does a rebalancing "premium" (or advantage) manifest itself over shorter time periods? As not everyone holds a portfolio for 40 years, is there a rebalancing benefit over 20-year periods? As shown in Table 6.2, the average ending total portfolio balance over 21 rolling periods of 20 years each was almost $3,500 higher in the annually rebalanced portfolio. This assumes an initial $1,428 investment into each of the

**Table 6.2    Average Ending Balance over 21 Periods of 20 Years (assuming a $1,428 initial investment in each of the seven assets)**

|  | Large-cap U.S. Equity ($) | Small-cap U.S. Equity ($) | Non-U.S. Equity ($) | U.S. Bonds ($) | Cash ($) | REIT ($) | Commodities ($) | Average Ending Portfolio Balance ($) |
|---|---|---|---|---|---|---|---|---|
| Annually Rebalanced | 14,218 | 13,999 | 13,378 | 13,576 | 13,240 | 13,887 | 13,851 | 96,149 |
| Buy-and-Hold | 18,712 | 19,550 | 14,517 | 7,699 | 5,315 | 15,514 | 11,363 | 92,670 |

seven assets. The ending bond and cash balances in the rebalanced portfolios were significantly higher than in the buy-and-hold portfolio. One obvious impact of rebalancing is that each asset has a similar ending account balance, not so with a buy-and-hold approach.

As shown in Figure 6.2, the annually rebalanced portfolio (shown by the line with triangles) had a higher ending account value in 15 out of 21 20-year rolling periods. The buy-and-hold portfolio 20-year ending account balances are shown by the line with circles. The first 20-year period was 1970 to 1989. The second covered 1971 to 1990, and so on. The x-axis indicates the ending year of each 20-year rolling period.

A buy-and-hold approach was superior during periods characterized by high returns and very few annual losses. Understandably, under those conditions a buy-and-hold approach will outperform. For example, the buy-and-hold portfolio outperformed the annually rebalanced portfolio over the 20-year period ending in 1994 (1975–1994) by roughly $15,000. During that particular 20-year period, the seven-asset portfolio had positive

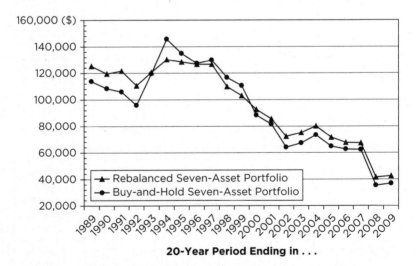

**20-Year Period Ending in . . .**

**Figure 6.2  Ending Portfolio Account Balances over Rolling 20-Year Periods**

returns in 19 of the 20 years. Moreover, in 14 of those years, the annual return was in excess of 10 percent. The lone annual loss was in 1990 and was only –3.26 percent.

If an investor could look forward and predict consistently positive returns for his or her portfolio, a buy-and-hold approach would be preferred. But, as already shown, in 71 percent of the 21-year periods between 1970 and 2009, a rebalanced portfolio generated superior performance.

A distinct benefit of rebalancing is that the terminal account values of the fixed income components (bonds and cash) are higher. When rebalancing annually, the average 20-year ending account value in bonds was over $13,500 and in cash just over $13,200 (from a $1,428 starting balance in both cases). Using a buy-and-hold approach, the average ending balance after 20 years in the bond fund was roughly $7,700 and the average terminal account value in the cash component was about $5,300 (see Table 6.2).

Why does this matter? Bonds and cash tend to have lower returns than equity and equity-like assets over long time frames. As a result, the bond and cash account balances become disproportional over time with the account balances of the equity components dominating the portfolio. This can be advantageous if, in the latter years of a portfolio, the equity-based assets perform well. But if equity and equity-like assets suffer declines, the investor can experience heavy losses because of the disproportionately large allocations in equity.

Of course, this problem is solved by rebalancing. When equity assets have strong annual gains, their excesses are diverted (i.e., rebalanced) to the fixed income components of the portfolio (bonds and cash). Because bonds and cash seldom have negative returns, the gains are preserved in a sort of fixed income safe haven. As investors age, having a safe haven for a portion of his or her portfolio becomes very appealing. Achieving a safe haven does not require that a portfolio be moved entirely to cash or bonds. Rather, systematic rebalancing goes a long way toward achieving it.

## Choosing a Schedule

Having demonstrated the virtues of rebalancing in a seven-asset portfolio over a 40-year period, let's now return to the 7Twelve portfolio.

The 7Twelve portfolio utilizes rebalancing on a periodic basis—monthly, quarterly, or annually based on the preference of the investor. Table 6.3 shows the annual returns of the 7Twelve portfolio from 2000 to 2009 using the three different rebalancing schedules.

### 7TWELVE

The 7Twelve portfolio utilizes rebalancing on a periodic basis—monthly, quarterly, or annually based on the preference of the investor.

**Table 6.3  The 7Twelve Portfolio's Annual Returns with Various Rebalancing Schedules**

| Year | Monthly Rebalancing (%) | Quarterly Rebalancing (%) | Annual Rebalancing (%) |
|------|------|------|------|
| 2000 | 6.35 | 6.05 | 6.78 |
| 2001 | −1.37 | −0.94 | −1.58 |
| 2002 | −1.06 | −0.66 | −0.68 |
| 2003 | 26.70 | 26.80 | 27.08 |
| 2004 | 17.76 | 17.79 | 17.73 |
| 2005 | 12.13 | 12.13 | 12.30 |
| 2006 | 15.40 | 15.35 | 15.38 |
| 2007 | 10.80 | 10.80 | 11.25 |
| 2008 | −25.70 | −24.87 | −24.62 |
| 2009 | 25.24 | 25.50 | 24.99 |
| 10-Year Average Annualized Return (%) | **7.52** | **7.73** | **7.81** |

As you can see, the performance differences are very slight. Therefore, rebalancing annually is (for most investors) the most logical. The results in Table 6.3 do not take into account trading commissions or taxation, both of which would negatively impact the performance of a portfolio that is being rebalanced more frequently, such as quarterly or monthly.

Let's quickly review what we've covered thus far. The 7Twelve design achieves the ultimate goal of an investment portfolio, which is to provide better performance with less risk. The 7Twelve "secret sauce" is very straightforward:

- *Broad diversification* through utilization of multiple asset classes (Chapters 3–4)
- *Low correlation* among the portfolio components (Chapter 5)
- *Strategic* rather than tactical management through periodic rebalancing (Chapter 6)

Chapter 7 discusses the mechanics of building a portfolio that is right for your lifecycle stage. And yes, there is a senior citizen discount—as you get older, we lower the risk!

7

# ADJUSTING THE SECRET SAUCE

Investing is a lifelong activity. A portfolio for a 35-year-old may not be appropriate when we are 55 years old. Very simply, an investor's portfolio should adjust over his or her lifespan so as to reduce risk of loss.

There are several asset allocation models used by financial planners. One simple allocation method that is popular with some advisors is "your age in bonds." Very simply, whatever a person's age is, that is the allocation he or she should have in bonds. The remainder of the portfolio would be invested in riskier assets such as stocks. For example, a 55-year-old may have 55 percent of his or her savings in bonds and the rest in a diversified stock portfolio. This allocation would change every year or every few years as the investor ages.

The concept of "your age in bonds" has the appeal of simplicity. But simplicity has a way of overlooking individual needs and circumstances. Building an appropriate portfolio requires a great deal of consideration of the individual needs and resources of the individual investor, differences that tend to be more profound later in life (at least from a portfolio design perspective).

For example, building a portfolio for a 35-year-old is very straightforward in nearly all cases—this person needs a portfolio that is primarily invested in equities, such as the 7Twelve portfolio. Most 35-year-olds have accumulation portfolios that look very similar. The situation is very different when people pass the age of 55 or so. Life situations can be very different. Some 62-year-olds have a lot of money saved, a generous pension, and very little debt. Other 62-year-olds have very little money saved, no pension, and a heavy debt load. Because of large differences that can exist among investors after the age of 55, portfolio design later in life (late accumulation phase and the post-retirement "distribution" phase) must be tailored to individual circumstances. To make this point, let's compare two groups of investors: 30-year-olds and 55-year-olds.

Most 30-year-olds are still at the beginning of their careers or perhaps making a first career change. They all have many years of work and savings ahead. Thirty-year-olds typically have very little in savings, which means the market gyrations have only a minor impact on their net worth. Accordingly, a 30-year-old should concentrate more on formulating a regular savings plan, and whatever money they do save should be largely invested in equity as long as the allocation does not exceed his or her tolerance for risk. Consequently, 70 percent in equity and 30 percent "your age in bonds" works fine for most 30-year-olds.

The range of financial situations for people at the age of 55 is much broader than when they were 30 years old. There are 55-year-olds who have accumulated significant wealth while others have accumulated very little. Some people are close to vesting in an employer pension while others are relying 100 percent on their own savings for retirement. Family status can be very diverse also. Some people are married, others divorced, others remarried, and still others never married. There are those caring for large families, some with small families, some with no family, and some with extended families, including helping out aging parents or other relatives.

Consequently, there is no typical 55-year-old. Each situation is unique, and his or her asset allocation needs to take into account a host of life situation variables.

## The Saving Years and the Spending Years

Investors need a portfolio that is designed to meet their needs in the accumulation phase of life. This phase typically occurs between age 25 to 65—the working and saving years. The ideal guideline is to invest 10 percent of your annual salary each year into a retirement portfolio, such as the 7Twelve portfolio. Shown below in Figure 7.1 is an example of how the 7Twelve accumulation portfolio grew over the 10 years from January 2000 to December 2009.

The starting balance at the beginning of the year 2000 was assumed to be $10,000. If that seems like too big a number, just roll with it and enjoy the analysis! The investment at the end of the first year was $1,000. Each additional end-of-year annual investment increased by 10 percent over the 10-year period.

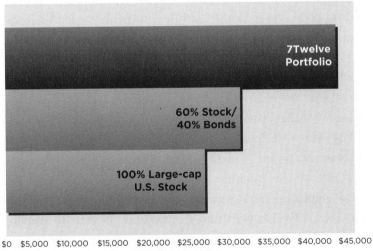

**Ending Account Balance**

**Figure 7.1  Performance Comparison in the *Accumulation* Phase**

The multi-asset 7Twelve portfolio had an ending balance of over $42,000. A simple two-asset portfolio (60 percent large-cap U.S. stock/40 percent bonds) had an ending balance of just over $30,000. Finally, a single-asset "portfolio" (which is an oxymoron because the word "portfolio" implies multiple assets) had a final balance of $25,700. Annual rebalancing in the 7Twelve portfolio and the 60/40 portfolio was assumed.

The 7Twelve portfolio is ideally suited for the accumulation phase because it is weighted more toward equity investments (stocks, real estate, and commodities), which have a higher return potential. The equity portion of the 7Twelve portfolio has eight components and represents about 65 percent of the portfolio allocation. The 7Twelve portfolio also has a diversified fixed income portion that represents 35 percent of the total portfolio allocation. The four fixed income funds stabilize the performance of the portfolio against the occasional erratic performance of equities.

Investors also need a portfolio that will meet their retirement income needs, which is referred to as the "distribution" phase. The distribution phase of an investor's life begins when money starts being withdrawn from your retirement account(s). This generally covers the time frame from age 65 to 85 (or later). In general terms, the accumulation phase can be as long as 40 to 45 years and the distribution phase can last up to 25 or even 35 years. The 7Twelve portfolio is an ideal portfolio for the distribution period, as shown in Figure 7.2.

The starting balance in this performance comparison was assumed to be $100,000. The first year's withdrawal was 5 percent of the balance, or $5,000. The annual cash withdrawal increased by 3 percent each year. As can be seen, the multi-asset 7Twelve portfolio dominated the 60/40 portfolio and the S&P 500 Index over the 10-year period of this performance comparison. After 10 end-of-year withdrawals, the 7Twelve portfolio had an ending balance of over $131,000,

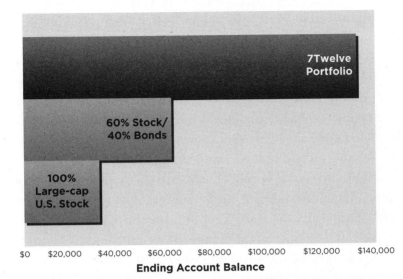

**Ending Account Balance**

**Figure 7.2   Performance Comparison in the *Distribution* Phase**

the 60/40 portfolio ending balance was $58,802, and the 100 percent large-cap U.S. stock portfolio ended with $29,902. Annual rebalancing in the 7Twelve portfolio and the 60/40 portfolio was assumed.

Every portfolio—whether it is a preretirement accumulation portfolio or a postretirement distribution portfolio—should have a diversified core component. The core may represent 100 percent, or 50 percent, or 10 percent of the investor's overall portfolio based upon the needs and preferences of the investor. Regardless of its allocation within the overall portfolio, the core should be diversified. Unfortunately, most portfolios are not built this way. As a result, most portfolios are underdiversified—at least in terms of diversification breadth.

The 7Twelve portfolio represents the diversified core that belongs in every portfolio, whether belonging to a 25-year-old or a 75-year-old. How much to allocate to the core is determined by life situation, or what has been referred to as "allocation age." As a general guideline, the portfolio allocation to the "core" should be in the range of 20 percent to 100 percent.

A young investor early in life could have a portfolio that is 100 percent 7Twelve. As you recall, the 7Twelve portfolio has overall allocation of about 65 percent to equities and 35 percent to fixed income—which represents a diversified balanced portfolio. This allocation creates more growth potential, without exposing the investor to uncompensated risk.

Alternatively, an investor late in life (perhaps during retirement) may have only a 20 to 30 percent allocation to a diversified core (such as the 7Twelve) with the balance invested in cash, TIPS, and/or annuities. Such an allocation would emphasize capital preservation rather than growth of capital.

Regardless of lifecycle stage, every investment portfolio is designed to achieve some level of growth and some level of capital preservation. Generally speaking, growth in the portfolio is the primary goal early in life and preservation of capital is the primary goal later in life.

## How Portfolio Mechanics Change in the Golden Years

One of the most difficult aspects of investing is determining how much risk to take in your portfolio at various stages of life. For instance, portfolio losses during the pre-retirement accumulation phase are easier to recover from than losses during the post-retirement distribution phase.

The mechanics of an investment portfolio are very different during the distribution phase. Losses in the portfolio are more difficult to recover from because withdrawals from the portfolio only serve to exacerbate (make worse) the losses. As shown in Table 7.1, a retirement "distribution" portfolio faces a much steeper climb to break-even after a loss than does an "accumulation" portfolio. As shown by the shaded boxes,

**Table 7.1   The Math of Recovery from Portfolio Losses**

| | Required Average Annual Percent Return to Restore Original Portfolio Balance after a Loss | | | | |
|---|---|---|---|---|---|
| | Distribution Portfolio* | | | | |
| Portfolio Loss (%) | Within 1 Year (%) | Within 2 Years (%) | Within 3 Years (%) | Within 4 Years (%) | Within 5 Years (%) |
| −5 | 16.8 | 11.1 | 9.3 | 8.4 | 8.0 |
| −10 | 23.7 | 14.4 | 11.5 | 10.1 | 9.4 |
| −15 | 31.4 | 18.0 | 13.9 | 12.0 | 10.9 |
| −20 | 40.2 | 22.0 | 16.5 | 14.0 | 12.5 |
| −25 | 50.2 | 26.4 | 19.4 | 16.1 | 14.3 |
| −30 | 61.8 | 31.3 | 22.6 | 18.5 | 16.2 |
| −35 | 75.3 | 36.9 | 26.1 | 21.2 | 18.4 |
| | Accumulation Portfolio** | | | | |
| Portfolio Loss (%) | Within 1 Year (%) | Within 2 Years (%) | Within 3 Years (%) | Within 4 Years (%) | Within 5 Years (%) |
| −5 | 5.3 | 2.6 | 1.7 | 1.3 | 1.0 |
| −10 | 11.1 | 5.4 | 3.6 | 2.7 | 2.1 |
| −15 | 17.6 | 8.5 | 5.6 | 4.1 | 3.3 |
| −20 | 25.0 | 11.8 | 7.7 | 5.7 | 4.6 |
| −25 | 33.3 | 15.5 | 10.1 | 7.5 | 5.9 |
| −30 | 42.9 | 19.5 | 12.6 | 9.3 | 7.4 |
| −35 | 53.8 | 24.0 | 15.4 | 11.4 | 9.0 |

*Distribution portfolio assumptions: $100,000 initial balance, first year withdrawal of 5 percent of initial balance, 3 percent increase in annual cash withdrawal.
**Accumulation portfolio assumptions: single lump sum investment with no additional investments.

an accumulation portfolio needs only an average annual return of 7.7 percent to recover from a 20 percent loss within three years.

A distribution portfolio in which money is being withdrawn each year must generate at least a 16.5 percent average annual return over a three-year period to recover from a 20 percent portfolio loss. This distribution portfolio assumes a starting balance of $100,000, an initial withdrawal at the end of the first year of 5 percent (in this case, $5,000), and an annual increase in the withdrawal of 3 percent. Thus, the second year withdrawal in this analysis was $5,150, and so on.

The conclusion we can draw from the information in Table 7.1 is quite clear: When building a distribution portfolio for the postretirement years, it is vitally important to avoid large losses. An investor's postretirement portfolio must be more loss resistant than the portfolio that was designed for his or her early accumulation years.

The 7Twelve portfolio (with four Life Stage allocation models) is ideally suited for both the accumulation phase and the distribution phase.

## Allocation Age versus Chronological Age

In general, it's more appropriate to create generic, all-purpose portfolio models for younger people and less appropriate to propose generic asset allocation models for older investors. Life has a way of introducing lots of sticky details as you grow older—and those details should have a bearing on your investment portfolio. Very simply, it is reasonable to aggregate the asset allocation needs of 30-year-olds without doing too much violence to their individual circumstances. But when dealing with investors over the age of 55, the plot has thickened and their individual circumstances need to be factored into their portfolio design.

Here is a solution: Determine a person's allocation age, rather than simply relying upon his or her chronological age. An investor's allocation age may be higher or lower than a person's chronological age depending on the individual investor. In a sense, the general rule of "your age in bonds" is a fair place to begin forming an asset allocation model, but asset

**7TWELVE**

Life has a way of introducing lots of sticky details as you grow older—and those details should have a bearing on your investment portfolio.

allocation adjustments should then be made up or down based on factors unique to each individual.

For example, consider two different 55-year-old investors. The first 55-year-old is barely getting by. All she has for retirement is the small amount she has saved in her 401(k). She has some housing debt and is caring for her aging parents, who are both in their 80s. She has the allocation age of 70 based on her life situation because she has very high cash-flow risk and is caring for elderly parents. She cannot afford to lose any sizable amount of her savings.

The second 55-year-old has a healthy and generous pension plan, no housing or consumer debt, a large Roth IRA account balance that is positioned very conservatively, and is expected to inherit a sizable estate in the next few years. Her allocation age is 40 because she has little cash-flow risk, no debt, and no foreseen future liabilities. (There is no magic formula to determine allocation age. It is a subjective evaluation. So in these two examples, I have simply illustrated that allocation age can often be different than chronological age.)

For these two investors the guideline is this: Start with the chronological age in bonds and then adjust the fixed income allocation to equal the allocation age. Recall that both investors have a chronological age of 55.

Let's test this approach in 2008. The first investor will have a 70 percent allocation to bonds in 2008 due to her tight financial situation, with the balance of the allocation (in this case, 30 percent) invested in the 7Twelve portfolio. The second investor will have a 40 percent allocation to bonds and a 60 percent 7Twelve allocation in 2008 because she is in a much better financial situation.

### 7TWELVE

Start with the chronological age in bonds and then adjust the fixed income allocation to equal the allocation age.

**Table 7.2  Allocation Age versus Chronological Age**

| Chronological Age of Investor | Risk Assessment Based on Life Situations | Allocation Age of Investor | Allocation- Age Portfolio | Portfolio Performance in 2008 (%) |
|---|---|---|---|---|
| 55 | Must take very little risk | 70 | 70% US Bonds 30% 7Twelve | −1.5 |
| 55 | Can accept higher risk | 40 | 40% US Bonds 60% 7Twelve | −11.4 |

Table 7.2 is a summary of how these two individuals fared in their respective "allocation-age" portfolios during 2008—a very rough year in case you've forgotten.

If both investors had a portfolio allocated according to their chronological age of 55, they both would have had a return of −6.5 percent in 2008 (based on an allocation model of 55 percent fixed income and 45 percent 7Twelve).

Taking into account life variables beyond simple chronological age, the risk-averse 55-year-old investor only lost 1.5 percent in 2008. The other 55-year-old investor (with an allocation age of a 40-year-old) experienced a bigger loss of 11.4 percent, but also has the prospect of outperforming during subsequent market rebounds.

## Life Stage Portfolios

A good portfolio also requires a thoughtful implementation plan over an investor's lifecycle. As we age, our tolerance for risk and volatility in our investment portfolio typically decreases. A simple risk-based implementation plan over an investor's lifecycle is "your age in bonds," where "allocation" age rather than simple "chronological" age determines the fixed income allocation.

Using "allocation age in bonds" as a starting point, let's now consider the 7Twelve Life Stage portfolios. The four Life Stage models are listed below and outlined in Table 7.3.

- Core 7Twelve Model
- 7Twelve Life Stage 50–60
- 7Twelve Life Stage 60–70
- 7Twelve Life Stage 70+

Each Life Stage model is different by virtue of increasing the allocation to inflation protected bonds and cash (both of which are assets that decrease the potential return of the portfolio but also decrease the potential loss). Inflation protected bonds are technically referred to as Treasury Inflation Protected Securities, or TIPS for short. Some investors may choose to use U.S. bonds instead of TIPS.

The "core" 7Twelve portfolio utilizes all 12 underlying mutual funds in equal allocations (8.33 percent) and is generally appropriate for investors up to the "allocation" age of 50. Some investors may choose to use the core, equally weighted 7Twelve portfolio throughout their entire lifespan based on a variety of personal financial circumstances.

The 7Twelve Life Stage 50–60 portfolio assigns an 80 percent allocation to the core Twelve portfolio, which translates to a 6.67 percent allocation to all twelve funds. The remaining 20 percent is divided equally between TIPS and cash. Thus, TIPs and cash each have a total allocation of 16.67 percent. Thus, the Life Stage 50–60 model has an allocation model of 80/10/10—80 percent to core Twelve and a 10 percent additional allocation to TIPS and cash—which translates to a general allocation model of approximately 50 percent equities and

**Table 7.3 7Twelve Life Stage Portfolios**

| Life Stage Portfolio → (based on "allocation age") | Core 7Twelve Model | 7Twelve Life Stage 50-60 | 7Twelve Life Stage 60-70 | 7Twelve Life Stage 70+ |
|---|---|---|---|---|
| **Approximate Asset Allocation Model (% equity / % fixed income)** | 65/35 | 50/50 | 40/60 | 25/75 |
| Generally appropriate for . . . | Investors in the age range of 20-50 | Investors in the age range of 50-60 | Investors in the age range of 60-70 | Investors in the age range of 70+ |
| Investment Objective | Early accumulation years, preretirement | Late accumulation years, preretirement | Early distribution period, postretirement | Late distribution period, postretirement |

**7Twelve Life Stage Asset Allocation Model**

| 7Twelve Mutual Funds | | Allocation to Each Equity Mutual Fund | | |
|---|---|---|---|---|
| Large-cap U.S. Stock | 8.33% | 6.67% | 5.0% | 3.33% |
| Midcap U.S. Stock | 8.33% | 6.67% | 5.0% | 3.33% |
| Small-cap U.S. Stock | 8.33% | 6.67% | 5.0% | 3.33% |
| Non-U.S. Stock | 8.33% | 6.67% | 5.0% | 3.33% |
| Emerging Markets | 8.33% | 6.67% | 5.0% | 3.33% |
| Real Estate | 8.33% | 6.67% | 5.0% | 3.33% |
| Natural Resources | 8.33% | 6.67% | 5.0% | 3.33% |
| Commodities | 8.33% | 6.67% | 5.0% | 3.33% |
| | | Allocation to Each Fixed Income Mutual Fund | | |
| U.S. Bonds | 8.33% | 6.67% | 5.0% | 3.33% |
| International Bonds | 8.33% | 6.67% | 5.0% | 3.33% |
| TIPS | 8.33% | 16.67% | 25.0% | 33.33% |
| Cash | 8.33% | 16.67% | 25.0% | 33.33% |

50 percent fixed income. (Again, U.S. bonds could be used in lieu of TIPS based upon the preference of the investor.)

The Life Stage 50–60 model is generally appropriate for investors from age 50 to 60. By increasing the allocation to TIPS and cash, the Life Stage 50–60 portfolio has reduced risk and slightly reduced return (as shown in Table 7.4).

The Life Stage 60–70 portfolio assigns an even higher allocation to TIPS and cash and is generally appropriate for investors from age 60 to 70. Its allocation model is 60/20/20 (60 percent allocation to core 7Twelve, 20 percent additional allocations to TIPS and cash). There is a 5 percent allocation to all of the 12 funds, except for TIPS and cash, which have a 25 percent allocation. The overall allocation model is 40 percent equities and 60 percent fixed income.

Finally, the Life Stage 70+ model assigns the highest allocation to TIPS and cash. Its allocation model is 40/30/30 (40 percent allocation to core 7Twelve and 30 percent additional allocations to TIPS and cash). This model is designed for investors who are age 70 and older. It is not meant to represent the definitive portfolio for investors of this age, but it is a reasonable general guideline. Each of the 12 funds has a 3.33 percent allocation, except for cash and TIPS, which have an allocation of 33.33 percent—which translates to an overall allocation model of 25 percent equities and 75 percent fixed income.

It's important to consider that the 7Twelve Life Stage models are just that—general models. Your individual circumstances may warrant a different model with a different allocation. The elegance of the 7Twelve approach allows you to implement a 7Twelve model that is most appropriate for you. This is accomplished by customizing the allocation to the 12 underlying assets in the 7Twelve portfolio. A customized investment portfolio can also be created by teaming the core 7Twelve model with other investment products, such as annuities.

The annual returns of each 7Twelve Life Stage Portfolio is reported in Table 7.4. Most people will immediately look at the performance of each portfolio in 2008—the year from hell. As you can see, the various 7Twelve portfolios behaved differently in 2008, just as they are designed to do. Also reported in Table 7.4 are the annual returns of the two-fund portfolio and the one-fund portfolio. It is worth noting that the most conservative 7Twelve Life Stage portfolio (70+) outperformed the two-fund 60/40 portfolio in 8 of the 10 years. Importantly, the Twelve Life Stage 70+ portfolio lost only 9.2 percent in 2008 compared to a loss of almost 19 percent in the two-asset 60/40 portfolio. The one-fund portfolio of 100 percent large-cap U.S. stock was gutted in 2008. This serves as a potent reminder that breadth of diversification (which a two-fund portfolio lacks) is particularly critical during the distribution phase. Annual rebalancing was assumed for the four different 7Twelve Life Stage portfolios as well as the two-fund (60/40) portfolio.

As demonstrated by the various 7Twelve Life Stage portfolios, reducing the risk in our portfolios as we age can be achieved by adjusting the asset allocation mix. For example, at age 50 (that is, "allocation" age of 50) an investor may wish to reduce the risk of his or her portfolio. If so, transitioning from the core equally weighted 7Twelve portfolio to the Life Stage 50–60 portfolio may be appropriate. This shift need not require a total portfolio transition because that would create an undesirable taxable event if the portfolio is not in a tax-sheltered account such as an IRA or 401(k).

The more tax-efficient way to transition from the core 7Twelve portfolio to the Life Stage 50–60 portfolio (and each subsequent 7Twelve Life Stage portfolio) is to simply direct additional investments (i.e., new investment dollars) to the TIPS (or U.S. bonds) and cash mutual funds that you already own. This will accomplish the needed "overweight" in these

**Table 7.4 Annual Returns of 7Twelve Life Stage Portfolios**

| Calendar Year* | Core 7Twelve Model (%) | 7Twelve Life Stage Portfolios | | | Comparison Portfolios | |
|---|---|---|---|---|---|---|
| | | 7Twelve Life Stage 50-60 (%) | 7Twelve Life Stage 60-70 (%) | 7Twelve Life Stage 70+ (%) | One-Fund Portfolio (100% large-cap U.S. stock) (%) | Two-Fund Portfolio (60% stock/40% bonds) (%) |
| 2000 | 6.78 | 7.35 | 7.92 | 8.49 | -9.70 | -1.22 |
| 2001 | -1.58 | -0.08 | 1.42 | 2.92 | -11.86 | -3.79 |
| 2002 | -0.68 | 1.26 | 3.19 | 5.13 | -21.50 | -8.85 |
| 2003 | 27.08 | 22.57 | 18.07 | 13.56 | 28.16 | 18.49 |
| 2004 | 17.73 | 15.13 | 12.52 | 9.91 | 10.69 | 8.10 |
| 2005 | 12.30 | 10.39 | 8.49 | 6.58 | 4.86 | 3.84 |
| 2006 | 15.38 | 12.82 | 10.26 | 7.70 | 15.80 | 11.16 |
| 2007 | 11.25 | 10.71 | 10.17 | 9.62 | 5.12 | 5.81 |
| 2008 | -24.62 | -19.47 | -14.32 | -9.18 | -36.70 | -18.66 |
| 2009 | 24.99 | 20.94 | 16.89 | 12.84 | 26.32 | 17.22 |
| 10-Year Annualized Return (2000-2009) | **7.81** | **7.49** | **7.07** | **6.57** | **-1.00** | **2.60** |
| 10-Year Std Dev of Annual Returns (2000-2009) | **15.11** | **12.17** | **9.27** | **6.47** | **20.90** | **11.63** |
| 10-Year Growth of $10,000 (2000-2009) | **$21,212** | **$20,582** | **$19,802** | **$18,893** | **$9,047** | **$12,921** |

*Assuming annual rebalancing.

two assets without having to sell portions of the other ten mutual funds. It may take a year or two to reach the desired 80/10/10 allocation specified in the Life Stage 50–60 model. That's okay. Recipes are flexible. So are portfolios.

In Chapter 8, we'll delve more deeply into the issue of portfolio preservation during retirement as we examine the classic question: "How long will my retirement nest egg last?"

CHAPTER 8

# HOW LONG WILL MY NEST EGG LAST?

Solving the retirement income puzzle has at least three components:

1. Investing adequately into your retirement accounts during your working career.
2. Withdrawing money from a retirement portfolio at a sustainable rate.
3. Utilizing a multi-asset portfolio design that properly balances goals for growth and capital preservation.

This chapter will focus on items two and three in this list. We will examine three different retirement withdrawal rates and four different retirement portfolios—one of which is a multi-asset portfolio.

The job of a retirement portfolio is to provide a modest return while protecting years of hard-earned savings. Therefore, protection of capital and growth of capital are simultaneous goals. However, during the retirement years, protecting your nest egg is the primary goal. Your retirement portfolio needs to carry you through your retirement years; therefore, it should not be exposed to too much risk.

Most retirement portfolios represent a blend of individual asset classes. A common blend is 60 percent stock and 40 percent fixed income. As already referred to in prior chapters, this particular mix is referred to as a 60/40 balanced fund.

Building a portfolio with only two assets is comparable to a diet of meat and potatoes. Just as we need diversity in our diet, we also need diversity in our investment portfolios.

As there are more investable equity asset classes than there were 40 years ago (such as real estate and commodities), a "balanced" portfolio should include more than one or two asset classes. This chapter will compare four different retirement portfolios:

1. 100 percent U.S. bonds
2. 100 percent large-cap U.S. stock
3. 60 percent large-cap U.S. stock/40 percent U.S. bonds
4. Multi-asset portfolio

The multi-asset portfolio is the same seven-asset portfolio that we've examined in prior chapters (large-cap U.S. stock, small-cap U.S. stock, non–U.S. stock, real estate, commodities, U.S. bonds, and cash). Each of the seven funds in the multi-asset portfolio was equally weighted and annually rebalanced. I would analyze the 7Twelve portfolio here if it had a 40-year history, but it doesn't. The seven-asset portfolio does have a 40-year performance history so it will represent the essence of the 7Twelve portfolio.

The performance of each portfolio will be tested during the distribution phase of an investor's lifecycle; that is, when money is being withdrawn during retirement.

## Survival of the Fittest

This analysis of various distribution portfolios is based on a $100,000 balance at the start of retirement and an annual cost of living adjustment (COLA) of 3 percent will be used for each. Three different initial withdrawal rates will be used: 5 percent, 7.5 percent, and 10 percent. The 5 percent withdrawal rate is associated with a $5,000 withdrawal in the first year of retirement and an annual increase each year of 3 percent. Thus, the second-year withdrawal is $5,150, the third year is $5,305, and so on. The 7.5 percent withdrawal rate is associated with a $7,500 first-year withdrawal, and 10 percent is a $10,000 first-year withdrawal. A 10 percent withdrawal rate is unusually high, but I'm conducting a stress test here— not advocating a high withdrawal rate.

The dollar amount of the starting balance ($100,000 in this case) is irrelevant. The portfolio survival rates are not affected by the size of the starting account balance. In other words, you could change the starting balance to $500,000 and it would not change the portfolio survival probabilities. Survival probability is determined by initial withdrawal rate and annual cost of living adjustment.

As shown in Table 8.1, each of the four portfolios survived all sixteen 25-year periods during the 40-year period between 1970 to 2009 assuming a 5 percent withdrawal rate (or $5,000 initial withdrawal with a 3 percent COLA). The term "survival" means that the distribution portfolio was not depleted within a 25-year period. A 25-year period simulates a retiree from age 65 (assumed retirement age) to age 90. The first 25-year period was from 1970 to 1994, the second was from 1971 to 1995, and so on.

If the retiree initially withdraws $7,500 (which equates to a 7.5 percent initial withdrawal rate) the survival rate of the

---

**7TWELVE**

The term "survival" means that the distribution portfolio was not depleted within a 25-year period.

---

all-bond portfolio and the all-stock portfolio slipped to 81 percent, meaning that those two investments survived only in 81 percent of the sixteen actual 25-year periods between 1970 and 2009.

Assuming a 7.5 percent initial withdrawal rate, the two-fund portfolio (60 percent large-cap U.S. stock/40 percent bond) survived 94 percent of the time, while the seven-fund (multi-asset) portfolio survived all sixteen historical 25-year periods.

If a retiree started into retirement with a 10 percent initial withdrawal rate, the outcome was ugly based on this historical portfolio survival analysis. The all-bond portfolio never survived any of the sixteen historical 25-year periods. That is, an all-bond portfolio was depleted before the retiree reached the age of 90 in every case. The 60/40 portfolio survived 63 percent of the

**Table 8.1  Average Probability of Portfolio Survival over Rolling 25-Year Periods (1970–2009)**

| Portfolio | 5% Withdrawal Rate $5,000 First-Year Withdrawal (%) | 7.5% Withdrawal Rate $7,500 First-Year Withdrawal (%) | 10% Withdrawal Rate $10,000 First-Year Withdrawal (%) |
|---|---|---|---|
| 100% Bonds | 100 | 81 | 0 |
| 100% Large-cap U.S. Stock | 100 | 81 | 69 |
| 60% Large-cap U.S. Stock/40% Bonds | 100 | 94 | 63 |
| Multi-Asset Portfolio* | 100 | 100 | 94 |

*Indexes used in analysis:
Large-cap U.S. stock: S&P 500 Index
Small-cap U.S. stock: Ibbotson Small Companies Index 1970–1978, Russell 2000 Index 1979–2009
Non–U.S. stock: MSCI EAFE Index
Real Estate: NAREIT Index 1970–1977, Dow Jones U.S. Select REIT Index 1978–2009
Commodities: S&P Goldman Sachs Commodities Index
U.S. Bonds: Ibbotson Interm. Term Govt. Bond Index 1970–1975, Barclays Capital Aggregate Bond Index 1976–2009
Cash: 3-Month Treasury bill

time and the all-stock portfolio survived 69 percent of the time. The multi-asset portfolio was the most durable distribution portfolio, surviving in 94 percent of the 25-year periods.

The ending account balance for each portfolio at the conclusion of each 25-year period is shown in Table 8.2. Recall that the starting balance in this distribution portfolio survival analysis was $100,000 and that sixteen rolling 25-year periods were analyzed over the time frame from January 1, 1970, to December 31, 2009.

The all-stock portfolio had dramatically different ending account balances based on the particular 25-year period

**Table 8.2 Ending Portfolio Balances at 5 Percent Withdrawal Rate**

| Distribution Period | | Ending Portfolio Balance* | | | |
|---|---|---|---|---|---|
| Starting Year | Ending Year | 100% Bonds ($) | 100% Large-cap U.S. Stock ($) | 60% Stock/40% Bonds ($) | Multi-Asset Portfolio ($) |
| 1970 | 1994 | 328,876 | 423,235 | 436,043 | 845,058 |
| 1971 | 1995 | 288,319 | 626,127 | 524,404 | 1,098,752 |
| 1972 | 1996 | 273,736 | 619,419 | 517,255 | 1,091,048 |
| 1973 | 1997 | 306,703 | 561,175 | 525,072 | 992,888 |
| 1974 | 1998 | 345,023 | 1,407,485 | 913,370 | 1,086,036 |
| 1975 | 1999 | 342,231 | 3,437,144 | 1,564,608 | 1,524,303 |
| 1976 | 2000 | 362,278 | 2,015,902 | 1,126,507 | 1,361,106 |
| 1977 | 2001 | 306,810 | 1,324,018 | 829,448 | 1,035,453 |
| 1978 | 2002 | 363,273 | 1,302,864 | 896,969 | 933,187 |
| 1979 | 2003 | 418,563 | 1,653,156 | 1,087,986 | 990,208 |
| 1980 | 2004 | 471,726 | 1,523,239 | 1,064,780 | 868,265 |
| 1981 | 2005 | 509,257 | 1,091,140 | 875,064 | 726,453 |
| 1982 | 2006 | 522,010 | 1,505,580 | 1,076,455 | 882,302 |
| 1983 | 2007 | 346,534 | 1,268,665 | 844,449 | 770,648 |
| 1984 | 2008 | 341,273 | 620,466 | 559,088 | 431,607 |
| 1985 | 2009 | 292,703 | 772,175 | 612,740 | 490,348 |
| Average Ending Balance | | **363,707** | **1,259,487** | **840,890** | **945,479** |

*$100,000 starting balance, 5% initial withdrawal rate ($5,000 first-year withdrawal), 3% annual COLA

being analyzed. Over the period from 1970 to 1994, the 100 percent large-cap U.S. stock portfolio (i.e., S&P 500 Index) ended with a $423,235 balance, whereas the period from 1975 to 1999 produced an ending balance in excess of $3.4 million. The ending balances in the other three portfolios were much more consistent from year to year. An all-stock portfolio is extremely sensitive to the timing of returns, which makes it a poor choice for a retirement portfolio. A retiree should not be betting their retirement on the timing of returns within a particular asset class.

The issue of timing is even more evident in Table 8.3, which illustrates the results of a 10 percent withdrawal rate. The 100

**Table 8.3   Ending Portfolio Balances at 10 Percent Withdrawal Rate**

| Distribution Period | | Ending Portfolio Balance* | | | |
|---|---|---|---|---|---|
| | | 100% | 100% Large- | 60% | Multi-Asset |
| Start | End | Bonds | cap U.S. | Stock/40% | Portfolio |
| Year | Year | ($) | Stock ($) | Bonds ($) | ($) |
| 1970 | 1994 | 0 | 0 | 0 | 0 |
| 1971 | 1995 | 0 | 0 | 0 | 154,294 |
| 1972 | 1996 | 0 | 0 | 0 | 100,758 |
| 1973 | 1997 | 0 | 0 | 0 | 9,975 |
| 1974 | 1998 | 0 | 0 | 0 | 207,442 |
| 1975 | 1999 | 0 | 1,515,694 | 369,162 | 641,900 |
| 1976 | 2000 | 0 | 482,318 | 71,016 | 512,834 |
| 1977 | 2001 | 0 | 124,473 | 0 | 331,247 |
| 1978 | 2002 | 0 | 488,260 | 161,782 | 324,835 |
| 1979 | 2003 | 0 | 749,337 | 319,589 | 320,974 |
| 1980 | 2004 | 0 | 656,145 | 334,107 | 185,566 |
| 1981 | 2005 | 39,023 | 289,677 | 202,827 | 56,731 |
| 1982 | 2006 | 82,228 | 706,317 | 424,404 | 212,923 |
| 1983 | 2007 | 0 | 537,019 | 233,380 | 139,702 |
| 1984 | 2008 | 0 | 212,704 | 123,223 | 18,853 |
| 1985 | 2009 | 0 | 320,772 | 154,191 | 48,317 |

*$100,000 starting balance, *10%* Initial Withdrawal Rate ($10,000 first-year withdrawal), 3% Annual COLA

percent large-cap U.S. stock portfolio failed to survive the first five 25-year periods. Then, in the sixth 25-year period being analyzed (from 1975–1999), the ending balance ballooned to over $1.5 million. The cause is obvious. In 1973 and 1974 the S&P 500 suffered losses of 14.7 percent and 26.5 percent respectively. A distribution portfolio that sustains losses early on will likely never recover, particularly when being subjected to a high withdrawal rate. Once the 25-year analysis period was beyond those two tough years (1973 and 1974) the all-large-stock portfolio performed much better. The multi-asset portfolio survived all but one 25-year distribution period under the heavy burden of a 10 percent withdrawal rate.

The length of each portfolio's survival is summarized in Table 8.4. The assumptions in Table 8.3 apply here also ($100,000 starting balance, 10 percent initial withdrawal rate, 3 percent cost of living increase in the annual cash withdrawal).

The average survival length of the 100 percent bond portfolio was 17.5 years. The 100 percent large-cap U.S. stock portfolio (the S&P 500 Index) and the 60/40 portfolio survived an average of just under 21 years. The multi-asset portfolio had an average survival length of 24.8 years. A retirement portfolio that can last at least 25 years means that a person who retires at age 65 has a viable retirement nest egg until they are 90 years old. That covers the life span of a majority of the world's population.

It's important to remember that this particular analysis studied distribution portfolio survival over multiple 25-year periods; thus the various portfolios either survived at least 25 years (the arbitrary maximum length in this analysis) or they were depleted before 25 years. The more important findings in Table 8.4 are the numbers less than 25. For example, a 65-year-old who retired in 1970 with a 100 percent bond retirement portfolio (and a 10 percent withdrawal rate and 3 percent COLA) ran out of money by 1984 (14 years later) at the

**Table 8.4   Number of Years Portfolio Survived at 10 Percent Withdrawal Rate**

| Distribution Period | | Number of Years Portfolio Survived* (25 years = maximum) | | | |
|---|---|---|---|---|---|
| Start Year | End Year | 100% Bonds | 100% Large-cap U.S. Stock | 60% Stock/40% Bonds | Multi-Asset Portfolio |
| 1970 | 1994 | 14 | 11 | 13 | 22 |
| 1971 | 1995 | 13 | 12 | 13 | 25 |
| 1972 | 1996 | 12 | 11 | 12 | 25 |
| 1973 | 1997 | 13 | 9 | 11 | 25 |
| 1974 | 1998 | 14 | 15 | 16 | 25 |
| 1975 | 1999 | 15 | 25 | 25 | 25 |
| 1976 | 2000 | 16 | 25 | 25 | 25 |
| 1977 | 2001 | 14 | 25 | 20 | 25 |
| 1978 | 2002 | 16 | 25 | 25 | 25 |
| 1979 | 2003 | 19 | 25 | 25 | 25 |
| 1980 | 2004 | 23 | 25 | 25 | 25 |
| 1981 | 2005 | 25 | 25 | 25 | 25 |
| 1982 | 2006 | 25 | 25 | 25 | 25 |
| 1983 | 2007 | 21 | 25 | 25 | 25 |
| 1984 | 2008 | 21 | 25 | 25 | 25 |
| 1985 | 2009 | 19 | 25 | 25 | 25 |
| Average Number of Years Portfolio Survived | | **17.5** | **20.8** | **20.9** | **24.8** |

*$100,000 starting balance, 10% Initial Withdrawal Rate ($10,000 first-year withdrawal), 3% Annual COLA

age of 79. Bummer. Even worse, had the 65-year-old invested in a 100 percent large-cap U.S. stock portfolio in 1970, they would have been out of money at the age of 76. A better solution would have been a multi-asset portfolio in 1970. The retiree account would have survived until they were 87 years old.

Clearly, in some of the 25-year periods, the various portfolios would have lasted longer than 25 years. For example, the 100 percent large-cap U.S. stock portfolio ended the 1975–1999 period with a balance of over $1.5 million (see Table 8.3).

With such a large ending balance after 25 years, it would be able to survive for many more years. The point of the results in Table 8.3 analysis is simply to demonstrate how often the various portfolios lasted *at least* 25 years (with 25 years being the maximum value). The real question answered by the results in Table 8.4 is "If the retirement distribution portfolio didn't last 25 years, how long did it last?"

As shown in Table 8.4, a multi-asset portfolio has been the most consistent in delivering at least 25 years of survival during the retirement distribution phase.

## Reviewing the Nest Egg Guidelines

Let's summarize by reviewing the guidelines that were presented at the start of this chapter. Building and utilizing a retirement portfolio has at least three components:

1. Investing adequately into your retirement accounts during your working career.
2. Withdrawing money from a retirement portfolio at a sustainable rate.
3. Utilizing a multi-asset portfolio design that properly balances goals for growth and capital preservation.

Investing 10 percent of your income during the accumulation years is a great goal and will typically be sufficient to adequately fund your retirement accounts. If you can't save 10 percent, save as much as you can. We can only do our best.

A 5 percent withdrawal rate with a 3 percent annual increase has been shown to be a sustainable rate during retirement. So, for example, if a 65-year-old has a $500,000 retirement nest egg at retirement, they would withdraw 5 percent the first year (or $25,000). The following year they would withdraw 3 percent more (or $25,750). The third-year withdrawal would be 3 percent more, or $26,523 . . . and so on.

Assembling a multi-asset portfolio creates a more durable retirement nest egg with a higher probability of surviving longer. We don't want our retirement portfolio to die before we do. A multi-asset approach is the best starting point to create a durable retirement portfolio. However, no portfolio, not even a multi-asset design, is capable of sustaining high withdrawal rates with a high probability of success. It's important to note that the retirement portfolio analysis in this chapter did not employ the "allocation age" technique described in the previous chapter. Your own particular circumstances will determine if that approach is suitable for you when designing and adjusting your retirement portfolio. In any case, a multi-asset strategy should be a significant component in your retirement portfolio.

Here is one suggestion about what not to do when building a distribution portfolio. The equity allocation within a retirement portfolio should *not* be increased in an effort to generate a higher return in order to make up for years of undersaving (i.e., the problem of investing too little during the accumulation years). Doing so dramatically increases timing risk—that is, the risk of experiencing negative returns in the early years of the distribution period and running out of money because the portfolio can't recover from the early losses.

The various 7Twelve Life Stage portfolios discussed in Chapter 7 (Table 7.3) represent appropriate retirement nest egg portfolios. In each Life Stage portfolio, the multi-asset 7Twelve portfolio is utilized—but in varying allocations according to the life stage and allocation age of the investor.

---

**7TWELVE**

We don't want our retirement portfolio to die before we do. A multi-asset approach is the best starting point to create a durable retirement portfolio.

---

The next three chapters explore popular nuances in portfolio design. Chapter 9 examines the "value versus growth" issue. Chapter 10 tackles the "active versus passive" topic, and Chapter 11 investigates target date funds versus balanced funds.

# SHOULD I TILT TOWARD VALUE OR GROWTH?

Whenever the topic of portfolio design is discussed, you can be sure that the issue of value investing versus growth investing will come up. It is an issue when considering how to invest in U.S. stock mutual funds and non-U.S. stock mutual funds, and possibly when selecting among real estate and resources mutual funds.

The 7Twelve portfolio can be assembled with a growth tilt (by using growth-oriented mutual funds) or a value tilt (by using value-oriented mutual funds). This chapter will provide guidance as you venture into the value-versus-growth debate.

The term *value* suggests that the investor is buying stock that is relatively less expensive, as opposed to stock that is relatively more expensive. The stock of a company that is classified as a "value stock" typically has a lower price-to-earnings ratio, which simply means that the stock currently has a lower price per share relative to the company's earnings per share. Think of it as investing in the home that needs repair versus putting more money down for the glitzy house on the hill. Very simply, value stocks are priced more attractively. The real question is whether or not value stocks tend to outperform growth stocks.

Growth stocks are just the opposite. They have higher price-to-earnings ratios; thus, an investor who purchases a growth stock is paying a higher price per share because he or she believes the stock price might go even higher.

Clearly, value and growth are relative measures. In fact, evaluating a stock's price (in value versus growth terms) is much like trying to determine if the price of a home you are interested in buying is priced right. Rather than wax philosophical, let's focus on the results of actual value and growth stock market indexes.

## Does It Make a Difference?

As reported in Table 9.1, the 30-year annualized return of growth-oriented large-cap U.S. stock was 9.75 percent (which represents the average of the Dow Jones Large Cap Growth Index and the Dow Jones U.S. Large Cap Growth Index). The Dow Jones U.S. indexes were formerly the "Wilshire" Indexes. The term *cap* is an abbreviation of *capitalization*. Capitalization is the way in which stocks are size classified (large-cap, midcap, small-cap). Capitalization is calculated by multiplying the current price of a stock by the number of shares that have been sold to investors.

The two value-oriented large-cap U.S. stock indexes in this study (Dow Jones Large Cap Value Index and Dow Jones U.S. Large Cap Value Index) had an average return of 11.58 percent over the period 1980–2009. Large-cap U.S. stock with a value orientation had a higher 30-year average return than large-cap U.S. stock with a growth orientation. This difference in favor of value is referred to as a *value premium*. There was a value premium among large-cap U.S. stocks, which translated into a total dollar premium of over $104,000 during this particular 30-year period.

The 30-year average annualized return of two midcap value indexes (Dow Jones Mid Cap Value and Dow Jones U.S. Mid

**Table 9.1 Annual Returns of Value and Growth U.S. Equity Indexes**

| Year | U.S. Large-cap Growth[1] (%) | U.S. Large-cap Value[2] (%) | U.S. Midcap Growth[3] (%) | U.S. Midcap Value[4] (%) | U.S. Small-cap Growth[5] (%) | U.S. Small-cap Value[6] (%) |
|---|---|---|---|---|---|---|
| 1980 | 39.70 | 24.88 | 47.89 | 23.56 | 48.71 | 22.58 |
| 1981 | –11.13 | 1.98 | –7.37 | 9.34 | –12.18 | 13.36 |
| 1982 | 16.49 | 20.47 | 21.79 | 26.05 | 19.91 | 31.35 |
| 1983 | 19.15 | 24.23 | 22.22 | 28.33 | 21.64 | 37.86 |
| 1984 | 1.59 | 10.98 | –7.60 | 3.47 | –11.33 | 7.80 |
| 1985 | 32.59 | 31.13 | 32.69 | 31.87 | 27.51 | 35.71 |
| 1986 | 15.51 | 19.90 | 10.47 | 15.60 | 8.79 | 14.36 |
| 1987 | 6.02 | 1.46 | 0.82 | 3.20 | –3.31 | –2.01 |
| 1988 | 13.45 | 22.39 | 12.01 | 19.31 | 21.01 | 26.47 |
| 1989 | 32.53 | 30.18 | 24.93 | 24.08 | 18.04 | 17.62 |
| 1990 | –0.73 | –6.34 | –9.21 | –10.83 | –14.73 | –17.45 |
| 1991 | 37.93 | 24.87 | 51.88 | 38.90 | 49.95 | 39.36 |
| 1992 | 4.25 | 9.44 | 11.12 | 17.82 | 13.99 | 22.71 |
| 1993 | 0.57 | 16.39 | 15.29 | 15.29 | 16.23 | 20.12 |
| 1994 | 3.37 | –1.73 | –2.94 | –2.43 | –2.28 | –1.81 |
| 1995 | 38.02 | 39.25 | 35.21 | 32.26 | 35.24 | 26.39 |
| 1996 | 23.59 | 22.53 | 15.65 | 22.42 | 10.71 | 24.66 |
| 1997 | 33.45 | 34.23 | 20.56 | 35.01 | 14.99 | 31.35 |
| 1998 | 42.15 | 16.66 | 9.43 | 5.04 | 5.34 | –4.18 |
| 1999 | 36.64 | 3.08 | 57.46 | –1.87 | 55.87 | 0.48 |
| 2000 | –28.11 | 8.62 | –21.75 | 26.85 | –21.32 | 19.24 |

*(Continued)*

119

**Table 9.1 (Continued)**

| Year | U.S. Large-cap Growth[1] (%) | U.S. Large-cap Value[2] (%) | U.S. Midcap Growth[3] (%) | U.S. Midcap Value[4] (%) | U.S. Small-cap Growth[5] (%) | U.S. Small-cap Value[6] (%) |
|---|---|---|---|---|---|---|
| 2001 | −23.02 | −5.75 | −15.43 | 6.55 | −8.27 | 12.75 |
| 2002 | −29.15 | −16.06 | −28.62 | −7.96 | −33.72 | −5.53 |
| 2003 | 28.49 | 28.21 | 43.52 | 35.05 | 49.76 | 45.26 |
| 2004 | 7.36 | 13.48 | 17.14 | 21.54 | 17.25 | 18.99 |
| 2005 | 4.84 | 5.42 | 15.61 | 8.17 | 9.23 | 5.99 |
| 2006 | 8.32 | 22.11 | 11.14 | 16.26 | 11.43 | 20.49 |
| 2007 | 11.50 | 2.21 | 14.13 | −4.14 | 10.22 | −7.96 |
| 2008 | −38.46 | −35.13 | −42.78 | −36.22 | −39.12 | −35.34 |
| 2009 | 37.98 | 15.67 | 46.57 | 36.43 | 40.69 | 41.13 |
| 30-Year Annualized Return | **9.75** | **11.58** | **10.72** | **13.24** | **9.35** | **13.77** |
| Std Dev of Return | **22.26** | **16.05** | **23.97** | **17.05** | **23.96** | **18.63** |
| Growth of $10,000 | **$163,032** | **$267,469** | **$211,990** | **$417,121** | **$146,148** | **$479,397** |

[1] Average of Dow Jones Large Growth Index and Dow Jones U.S. Large Cap Growth Index.
[2] Average of Dow Jones Large Value Index and Dow Jones U.S. Large Cap Value Index.
[3] Average of Dow Jones Mid Growth Index and Dow Jones U.S. Mid Cap Growth Index.
[4] Average of Dow Jones Mid Value Index and Dow Jones U.S. Mid Cap Value Index.
[5] Average of Dow Jones Small Growth Index and Dow Jones U.S. Small Cap Growth Index.
[6] Average of Dow Jones Small Value Index and Dow Jones U.S. Small Cap Value Index.

Cap Value) was 13.24 percent, considerably better than the 10.72 percent average return of the combined midcap growth indexes. The difference in performance amounted to a value premium of over $205,000.

Among small-cap U.S. equity indexes, the value premium over the 30-year period was an astonishing 442 basis points (bps); that is, a 30-year value return of 13.77 percent minus a 30-year growth return of 9.35 percent equals a value premium of 442 bps. With a 30-year annualized return of 13.77 percent, small-cap value turned $10,000 into $479,397, or $333,249 more than the ending balance in small-cap growth.

The annual returns in Table 9.1 reflect performance from one point-in-time (January 1, 1980) to another point-in-time (December 31, 2009). Clearly, many investors won't invest for that length of time or that specific period of years, so it's useful to examine performance in smaller time frames, such as five-year periods. The performance premium for the value indexes and growth indexes are calculated in rolling five-year periods of time and are reported in Table 9.2.

The premium (whether growth or value) for each five-year period is shown in basis points. For instance, over the five-year period from 1980 to 1984, large-cap value U.S. equity demonstrated a 432 bps premium over large-cap growth U.S. equity. Among midcap U.S. equities during the same period, there was a value premium of 422 bps. Among small caps, the five-year value premium from 1980 to 1984 was 1,110 bps.

A few words about basis points. There are 100 basis points in one percentage point. For example, Fund A has a return of 10 percent and Fund B has a return of 11 percent. The 11 percent return of Fund B is 100 bps higher than the 10 percent return of Fund A. Or if Fund A has a return of 10 percent and Fund B has a return of 10.01 percent, Fund B has a higher return by 1 bps. The basis point measurement system is the clearest way to compare returns.

**Table 9.2  Value and Growth Premiums over 5-Year Rolling Periods**

| 5-Year Period | U.S. Large-Cap Equity | | U.S. Midcap Equity | | U.S. Small-Cap Equity | |
|---|---|---|---|---|---|---|
| | Growth[1](bps) | Value[2](bps) | Growth[3](bps) | Value[4](bps) | Growth[5](bps) | Value[6](bps) |
| 1980–1984 | | 432 | | 422 | | 1,110 |
| 1981–1985 | | 662 | | 819 | | 1,693 |
| 1982–1986 | | 452 | | 556 | | 1,241 |
| 1983–1987 | | 260 | | 509 | | 1,007 |
| 1984–1988 | | 337 | | 532 | | 818 |
| 1985–1989 | 15 | 96 | | 277 | | 388 |
| 1986–1990 | | | | 228 | | 152 |
| 1987–1991 | 330 | | 63 | | 118 | |
| 1988–1992 | 118 | 44 | | 18 | | 18 |
| 1989–1993 | | | 130 | | 9 | |
| 1990–1994 | 29 | | 98 | | | 9 |
| 1991–1995 | | 123 | 111 | | 71 | |
| 1992–1996 | | 330 | | 228 | | 377 |
| 1993–1997 | | 243 | | 360 | | 519 |
| 1994–1998 | 602 | | | 263 | | 214 |

| Period | 1 | 2 | 3 | 4 | 5 | 6 |
|---|---|---|---|---|---|---|
| 1995–1999 | 1,217 | | 897 | 831 | | 304 |
| 1996–2000 | 160 | | | | | 485 |
| 1997–2001 | | 312 | | | | 889 |
| 1998–2002 | | 599 | | | | 1,098 |
| 1999–2003 | | 979 | | | 314 | 2,056 |
| 2000–2004 | | 1,615 | | 346 | 684 | 1,121 |
| 2001–2005 | | 859 | | 112 | 912 | 864 |
| 2002–2006 | | 737 | | 139 | 919 | |
| 2003–2007 | | 207 | 517 | | 1,988 | |
| 2004–2008 | | 287 | 102 | | 849 | |
| 2005–2009 | 172 | | 325 | | 466 | |
| **Percent of Periods With "Premium"** | **31** | **69** | **31** | **27** | **69** | **73** |
| **Average Premium (bps)** | **330** | **476** | **121** | **118** | **488** | **818** |

[1] Average of Dow Jones Large Growth Index and Dow Jones U.S. Large Cap Growth Index.
[2] Average of Dow Jones Large Value Index and Dow Jones U.S. Large Cap Value Index.
[3] Average of Dow Jones Mid Growth Index and Dow Jones U.S. Mid Cap Growth Index.
[4] Average of Dow Jones Mid Value Index and Dow Jones U.S. Mid Cap Value Index.
[5] Average of Dow Jones Small Growth Index and Dow Jones U.S. Small Cap Growth Index.
[6] Average of Dow Jones Small Value Index and Dow Jones U.S. Small Cap Value Index.

As shown at the bottom of Table 9.2, large-cap value demonstrated a performance premium 69 percent of the time. The average five-year value premium was 476 bps. Conversely, large-cap growth outperformed large-cap value 31 percent of the time by an average of 330 bps.

Among midcap equity indexes, value also outperformed growth 69 percent of the time by an average of 488 bps (over five-year periods). When growth outperformed value (31 percent of the time), the margin of victory averaged 121 bps. Among midcap U.S. stocks, a value tilt has historically provided better performance than a growth tilt.

Among small-cap U.S. equity indexes, value beat growth 73 percent of the time by an average of 818 basis points (again, over five-year periods). However, when small-cap growth outperforms (27 percent of the time), the difference can be large. For example, during the five-year period of 1995–1999, small-cap growth beat small-cap value by 831 bps. Overall, however, when small growth outperformed small-cap value, the average margin of victory was only 118 bps.

These results do not argue for eliminating growth-oriented assets from a portfolio. However, this analysis does suggest that a value "tilt" is justified in the long run. If you are going to overweight your portfolio in one direction or the other, the overweight would be toward value stocks and value-oriented mutual funds/exchange traded funds.

The long-run advantage of a value tilt is illustrated in Table 9.3. As the length of the investing period increases (from one-year rolling periods to three-year rolling periods to five-year rolling periods to 10-year rolling periods), the frequency of a value premium increases.

For example, between 1980 and 2009, large-cap value indexes outperformed large-cap growth indexes 71 percent of the time over the 28 three-year rolling periods. Over twenty-one rolling 10-year periods, large value beat large growth

**Table 9.3  Frequency of a Value Premium**

|  | Frequency of Value Premium among Stocks | | |
| --- | --- | --- | --- |
| Rolling Time Periods (1980–2009) | U.S. Large-cap Stock (%) | U.S. Midcap Stock (%) | U.S. Small-cap Stock (%) |
| 30 One-Year Periods | 57 | 60 | 67 |
| 28 Three-Year Periods | 71 | 64 | 68 |
| 26 Five-Year Periods | 69 | 69 | 73 |
| 21 Ten-Year Periods | 86 | 95 | 95 |

86 percent of the time. Among small-cap indexes, small-cap value outperformed small-cap growth in 68 percent of the three-year rolling periods, but 95 percent of the time over rolling 10-year periods.

## The 7Twelve's Value Bias

The 7Twelve portfolio can be designed with a value or growth orientation. Based on this analysis, building a value-tilt into the 7Twelve portfolio is advisable. Not all of the mutual funds (or exchange traded funds) in the 7Twelve portfolio come in value or growth flavors. Where a value tilt can be achieved is by selecting value-oriented mutual funds in the U.S. equity category (three stock funds) and non–U.S. equity category (two stock funds). There are two other funds in the 7Twelve portfolio that have the potential to be value or growth tilted, that being the real estate fund and the resources fund. So anywhere from five to seven of the ingredients in the 7Twelve portfolio can have a bias toward value.

If history repeats, a value tilt in your portfolio should reward you with higher and more consistent returns. Understandably, a value-oriented portfolio will occasionally underperform when growth stocks have their day in the spotlight. It really boils down to what you, as an investor, really want. If you want steady performance, a value tilt is the right approach.

If you want to maximize those moments when equity markets make big gains, then growth is for you. A logical approach is to build a portfolio that has elements of both growth and value, but tilts toward value.

As shown in Table 9.4, the 7Twelve portfolio does exactly that. Among the equity funds in the 7Twelve portfolio, about 39 percent of their allocation is in value stocks, roughly 37 percent is allocated to stocks that are classified as "core" and 24 percent is committed to growth stocks. This allocation can shift somewhat over time, but in principle the 7Twelve portfolio will typically have a bent toward value.

In terms of market-cap focus, about half of the equity holdings in the 7Twelve portfolio are large-cap stocks, 31 percent are midcap stocks, and 20 percent are small-cap stocks.

The equity style labeled as "core" refers to stock that falls in between a value classification and a growth classification using Morningstar criteria. (Morningstar is an investment data provider headquartered in Chicago, Illinois.)

The results of this value versus growth comparison might have been different had different indexes been used, such as S&P Indexes, Morningstar Indexes, or Russell Indexes. Dow Jones and Dow Jones U.S. Indexes (formerly Wilshire Indexes) were chosen because they have the longest performance histories within the six style categories in this study (large growth, large value, mid-growth, mid value, small growth, and small value).

**Table 9.4   7Twelve Portfolio Value/Growth Allocations**

|  | Equity Style | | | |
| --- | --- | --- | --- | --- |
|  | Value | Core | Growth | Total |
| Large-Cap Equity | 19 | 17 | 13 | 49 |
| Midcap Equity | 10 | 13 | 8 | 31 |
| Small-Cap Equity | 10 | 7 | 3 | 20 |
| Total | 39 | 37 | 24 | |

The performance of "actively" managed value and growth funds has not been accounted for in this analysis. This analysis used performance data from market indexes, which are typically considered a "passive" approach to investing.

In fact, the next chapter, Chapter 10, discusses the issue of actively managed funds versus passively managed funds—another common debate among investors.

CHAPTER

# SHOULD I JUMP IN OR LET THE POT SIMMER?

The 7Twelve portfolio recipe calls for mutual funds as the ingredients. The ingredients can be actively managed mutual funds or passively managed mutual funds. (Exchange-traded funds (ETFs) can be used in place of or in combination with mutual funds at your discretion.)

In fact, the universe of mutual funds can roughly be divided into two camps: actively managed funds and passively managed index funds. ETFs are classified as passively managed index funds. The real world of investing isn't quite that simple, but such a division provides a reasonable starting point for this discussion.

An actively managed fund is one in which the fund manager has discretion in the selection of investments (e.g., stocks, bonds, cash, and so on) and how long investments are held in the portfolio.

Conversely, a passively managed mutual fund or ETF is typically mimicking a specific stock or bond market "index"; hence, they are referred to as *index funds*. An index fund manager is constrained to hold the same stocks or bonds as the underlying index that is being replicated. Passively managed funds tend to have lower expense ratios and turnover ratios than actively managed funds. The expense ratio of a mutual fund (or ETF) represents a portion of the costs of the management of the fund and is borne directly by the investor. Turnover ratio is a measure of how long a particular stock or bond is held in the fund's portfolio. Higher turnover is associated with higher expense ratios.

There is currently, and will always be, a debate regarding which approach is better: active or passive mutual funds. It's a worthwhile debate but difficult to definitively settle inasmuch as some actively managed funds outperform index funds and vice versa. It really comes down to philosophy: Do you believe that a passive approach to investing is a more compelling approach on the basis of cost efficiency and replication of core market indexes, *or* do you believe that there are money managers out there who have skill sufficient to beat passively managed index funds? Sounds like the nature versus nurture argument, which is another debate I can't solve!

## To Stir or Not to Stir?

The active versus passive debate always focuses on how individual mutual funds are managed, but another dimension of the active-passive issue is how frequently an investor manages his own portfolio of mutual funds. Does the chef know when to leave the recipe alone?

Active and passive investing takes place on at least two levels. The actual portfolio ingredients can be active or passive, and the management of the portfolio itself can be active or passive. In other words, investors can build their portfolios with actively managed or passively managed funds and then investors can manage those funds actively or passively.

---

### 7TWELVE

Active and passive investing takes place on at least two levels. The actual portfolio ingredients can be active or passive, and the management of the portfolio itself can be active or passive.

---

For example, if an investor is frequently moving money between the various index funds in his or her portfolio, the investor is an active investor using passively managed index funds or ETFs. On the other hand, if an investor purchases actively managed mutual funds but has a buy-and-hold approach within his or her portfolio, it could be argued that that individual is a passive investor using actively managed funds.

Table 10.1 illustrates the four possibilities in this expanded view of the active-passive debate in which two dimensions are considered instead of only one:

- The first dimension is the classic focus: Are the actual mutual funds actively or passively managed?
- The second dimension is rarely considered, that is: How does the investor manage his or her portfolio of funds— actively or passively?

The four active-passive combinations in Table 10.1 represent a simplified view of all possible combinations of active/passive at the individual mutual fund level and active-passive at the portfolio management level. There are surely many other possibilities. Thus, it is best to consider the information in Table 10.1 as a big picture *starting point for thoughtful discussion* rather than a summary of "how all things in the universe actually work."

**Table 10.1 Active versus Passive Grid**

| | Investor Using Passively Managed Index Funds or ETFs | Investor Using Actively Managed Mutual Funds |
|---|---|---|
| Passive Portfolio Management by Investor | **Passive-Passive:** Buy-and-hold index funds or ETFs | **Active-Passive:** Buy-and-hold actively managed funds |
| Active Portfolio Management by Investor | **Passive-Active:** Actively manage index funds or ETFs | **Active-Active:** Actively manage actively managed funds |

This *starting point* attempts to highlight a very fundamental question: Should index funds be passively managed by the investors that use them in their portfolios? If an investor actively manages a portfolio of index funds, isn't that incongruent with the passive nature of the funds being utilized? On the flip side, if an investor utilizes actively managed funds in his or her portfolio, does that give them the green light to actively manage those funds?

The bottom line is really this: The portfolio management style of the investor should be consistent with the type of mutual funds being utilized in his portfolio.

Let me suggest a simple guideline that will allow us to sidestep the unnecessary contention that accompanies the active-passive debate: Build the 7Twelve portfolio using actively managed funds if that is your preference *or* build the 7Twelve portfolio using passive index funds and/or ETFs if you prefer a passive approach to investing. Either way, you have a broadly diversified combination of mutual funds. If you want to actively manage the 7Twelve portfolio, you can rebalance each fund on a monthly basis. Alternatively, if you want to manage the 7Twelve portfolio more passively, you can rebalance annually. As shown in Table 6.3 in Chapter 6, rebalancing more frequently produces somewhat lower returns, but it makes active investors feel better that they are making the decisions. I will remind you that, historically, annual rebalancing has generated modestly better performance.

---

### 7TWELVE

The portfolio management style of the investor should be consistent with the type of mutual funds being used.

---

# The 7Twelve Works Both Ways

Now, let's take a look (for the first time) at how the performance of an "active" 7Twelve portfolio compares to a "passive" 7Twelve portfolio. Thus far in the book, all 7Twelve portfolio performance figures have reflected the passive 7Twelve portfolio using annual rebalancing, which by the way is a passive-passive approach.

The annual performance of the active 7Twelve portfolio and the passive 7Twelve portfolio (using monthly and annual rebalancing) are shown in Table 10.2. The active 7Twelve portfolio uses 12 actively managed funds and the passive 7Twelve

**Table 10.2   Active 7Twelve and Passive 7Twelve Returns**

| Year | Monthly Rebalancing | | Annual Rebalancing | |
|---|---|---|---|---|
| | Active 7Twelve Portfolio (%) | Passive 7Twelve Portfolio (%) | Active 7Twelve Portfolio (%) | Passive 7Twelve Portfolio (%) |
| 2000 | 10.91 | 6.35 | 11.71 | 6.78 |
| 2001 | 3.21 | −1.37 | 3.13 | −1.58 |
| 2002 | 2.21 | −1.06 | 2.27 | −0.68 |
| 2003 | 28.28 | 26.70 | 28.84 | 27.08 |
| 2004 | 19.72 | 17.76 | 19.86 | 17.73 |
| 2005 | 12.93 | 12.13 | 13.16 | 12.30 |
| 2006 | 16.37 | 15.40 | 16.36 | 15.38 |
| 2007 | 13.33 | 10.80 | 13.79 | 11.25 |
| 2008 | −29.84 | −25.70 | −28.22 | −24.62 |
| 2009 | 32.13 | 25.24 | 32.46 | 24.99 |
| 3-Year Annualized Return | **1.66** | **1.02** | **2.66** | **1.58** |
| 5-Year Annualized Return | **6.66** | **5.93** | **7.33** | **6.31** |
| 10-Year Annualized Return | **9.51** | **7.52** | **9.99** | **7.81** |

portfolio uses 12 passively managed exchange traded funds (ETFs). ETFs are, by definition, index funds because they mimic a chosen index. Monthly performance updates for the Active and Passive 7Twelve portfolios that I've assembled are available on my website (www.7TwelvePortfolio.com). By necessity, the monthly performance update assumes monthly rebalancing.

As you examine the performance of the active 7Twelve portfolio, you will notice that it outperformed the passive 7Twelve portfolio every year except 2008. The performance advantage is not always large, but a consistent active "premium" is evident. So, do I (the architect of the 7Twelve) favor the active 7Twelve portfolio? Nope. I actually prefer the pure logic of using passively managed exchange-traded funds and/or passively managed index-based mutual funds. I recognize that some "active" mutual fund managers are more capable than others—and they can outperform passively managed index funds.

However, and this is a key point, the only "active" aspect of the active 7Twelve portfolio is that it uses actively managed mutual funds. There is no attempt to add another layer of active (or tactical) management to the active 7Twelve portfolio. For example, there is no market timing taking place or tactical overweighting of the 12 underlying mutual funds. The only active component is the use of actively managed funds.

Rebalancing is the only management "tool" applied to the 7Twelve portfolio, whether using the active or the passive model. Of course, rebalancing is completely strategic—meaning that it is non-reactive to market conditions. It simply occurs on a schedule, no matter what stock or bond markets are doing or not doing. The 7Twelve portfolio is completely strategic, meaning that the portfolio ingredients as well as the rules of operation are known in advance and are completely transparent. The 7Twelve portfolio is *not* a tactical portfolio. It does not change the rules midstream because of market behavior.

# But If You *Still* Can't Decide . . .

I propose that the active-passive debate has been resolved. But if you really can't decide which way to go . . . do both. Build an active 7Twelve portfolio *and* a passive 7Twelve portfolio and have them compete against each other. Either way you win because you will have two well-diversified portfolios—which is more relevant to success than whether or not you are an "active" or "passive" investor.

The next chapter reviews two important mutual fund categories: target date funds and balanced funds—and how the 7Twelve portfolio compares to them. If you have a 401(k) or 403(b) retirement account, you'll want to read the next chapter very carefully.

CHAPTER

# A BETTER 401(K)

For many investors, their 401(k) retirement plan will represent the bulk of their retirement nest egg. There are two prominent types of mutual funds found in nearly every 401(k) "menu": target date funds and balanced funds. This chapter helps you make sense of them and better understand how the 7Twelve portfolio compares.

The United States Department of Labor (DOL) has issued opinions about the design of age-appropriate investments for investors in the Pension Protection Act of 2006. In general, the DOL guidelines suggest higher allocations to stock mutual funds for younger investors. As investors age, their portfolios should be exposed to less risk, meaning that the allocation to stock funds should be reduced and the allocation to bond funds should increase—very simply, higher risk–higher return portfolios early in life and lower risk–lower return portfolios later in life. Like I mentioned earlier, this stuff isn't rocket science.

## Switching the Default

Prior to the Pension Protection Act of 2006, the DOL felt that too many young investors had their 401(k) balances invested in money market mutual funds or stable value funds and, as a result, were missing needed growth potential in their retirement portfolios. In many cases this was true, and action to remedy this was warranted. (Stable value funds have low risk, but also low return.)

The remedy was to encourage the use of balanced funds or target date funds as the "default" funds instead of cash funds and stable value funds. Thus, in recent years the pendulum swung from a low-risk default investment product (money market mutual funds and stable value funds) to a higher-risk default investment product (target date funds and balanced funds). For young investors with a long investing horizon in front of them, this has been a useful evolution. For some older investors with only a few years separating them from retirement, this transition has been catastrophic. The issue, as is always the case, is timing. But more than that, it is also involves a misalignment between product design and usage.

The model governing the allocation to stocks and bonds over the lifecycle of an investor has been referred to as a portfolio "glide path." Naturally, there are many and varied opinions about how to design the ideal glide path.

Let's take a look at target date funds and balanced funds and then compare their performance with the 7Twelve portfolio.

## Introducing Target Date Funds and Balanced Funds

The "glide path" (or dynamic asset allocation model) in a target date fund produces a more risky portfolio with higher return potential when the target date is far in the future and a less risky portfolio as the target date nears (see Table 11.1). (The "target date" typically represents the year (or close to it) that the investor plans to retire.) For example, as of January 2010, the average 2040 target date fund had an asset allocation of approximately 85 percent in equity funds and 15 percent

**Table 11.1  Target Date Funds, Balanced Funds, and the 7Twelve Portfolio**

| Age of Investor in 2010 | Years to Retirement (at age 65) | Year of Retirement (target date) | Asset Allocation Model (% stock / % bonds) | | |
|---|---|---|---|---|---|
| | | | Target Date Fund | Balanced Fund | 7Twelve Life Stage Portfolios |
| 35 | 30 | 2040 | 85/15 | 60/40 | 65/35 |
| 45 | 20 | 2030 | 80/20 | 60/40 | 65/35 |
| 55 | 10 | 2020 | 65/35 | 60/40 | 50/50 |
| 65 | 0 | 2010 | 50/50 | 60/40 | 40/60 |
| 75 | 10 years ago | 2000 | 35/65 | 60/40 | 25/75 |

in fixed income funds. The average 2030 target fund allocation was roughly 80 percent stocks and 20 percent bonds. The average 2020 fund asset allocation model was generally about 65 percent stocks and 35 percent bonds, and the average 2010 fund had a 50/50 allocation.

The typical balanced fund has an asset allocation model that is approximately 60 percent stocks and 40 percent bonds. The performance of a 60/40 asset allocation model has been repeatedly referred to in this book. The 60/40 allocation model is the design of balanced mutual funds such as Dodge & Cox Balanced, T. Rowe Price Balanced, Vanguard Wellington, Fidelity Puritan, and many others. In fact, there are about 125 balanced funds in the mutual fund marketplace. Balanced funds don't employ a dynamic asset allocation model (i.e., glide path); rather they maintain a constant 60/40 allocation.

## The 7Twelve Portfolio Approach

As illustrated in Table 11.1, the 7Twelve portfolio has a more conservative asset allocation model than the average target date fund at every age. Compared to the typical balanced fund, the 7Twelve portfolio asset allocation is similar for young investors but considerably more conservative as the investor ages. The real deal is, of course, performance. Talk all you want, but how does the portfolio perform?

The performance of target date funds will be represented by the Fidelity Freedom funds. The lineup of Fidelity Freedom target date funds possesses roughly half of all the money invested in target date funds.

In Table 11.2 the performance of the Fidelity Freedom 2010 fund is shown alongside the Fidelity Balanced fund

Table 11.2   Target Retirement Year 2010 (Annual % Returns)

| Year | Investor Age | Fidelity Freedom 2010 Target Fund (FFFCX) (%) | Fidelity Balanced (FBLAX) (%) | 7Twelve Life Stage Portfolios* (%) |
|---|---|---|---|---|
| 2000 | 55 | 0.67 | 5.32 | 7.35 |
| 2001 | 56 | −4.34 | 2.25 | −0.08 |
| 2002 | 57 | −6.85 | −8.50 | 1.26 |
| 2003 | 58 | 17.13 | 28.24 | 22.57 |
| 2004 | 59 | 7.28 | 10.94 | 15.13 |
| 2005 | 60 | 5.92 | 10.68 | 8.49 |
| 2006 | 61 | 9.46 | 11.65 | 10.26 |
| 2007 | 62 | 7.43 | 8.99 | 10.17 |
| 2008 | 63 | −25.32 | −31.31 | −14.32 |
| 2009 | 64 | 24.82 | 28.05 | 16.89 |
| 3-Year Average Annualized Return | | **0.04** | **−1.40** | **3.33** |
| 5-Year Average Annualized Return | | **3.03** | **3.45** | **5.71** |
| 10-Year Average Annualized Return | | **2.73** | **5.20** | **7.30** |
| 10-Year Growth of $10,000 | | **$13,087** | **$16,607** | **$20,230** |

*7Twelve Life Stage 50 to 60 Portfolio from age 55–59; 7Twelve Life Stage 60–70 Portfolio from ages 60 to 64.

(one of the largest balanced funds) and the 7Twelve portfolio (using Life Stage 50–60 from age 55 to 59 and Life Stage 60–70 from age 60–64). The investor in this analysis was 55 years in 2000 and 65 years old in the year 2010; hence, the target retirement date of 2010.

During the first three years of the past decade (2000–2002), the 7Twelve Life Stage 50–60 Portfolio dominated the performance of the Fidelity 2010 target fund. The year 2002 was the worst year for the target date fund, with a loss of nearly 7 percent. The Fidelity Balanced fund did even worse, with a loss of 8.5 percent. The 7Twelve Life Stage 50–60 portfolio had a positive return of 1.26 percent in 2002. During the next five years, the equity markets were good to investors and all three portfolios had strong positive returns, though Fidelity Freedom 2010 lagged behind the other two. Then in 2008 all three portfolios were stress tested beyond expectations.

The Fidelity 2010 fund lost over 25 percent in 2008 despite being within 24 months of the stated target date. The Fidelity Balanced fund was hit even harder, with a loss of over 31 percent. The 7Twelve Life Stage 60–70 portfolio lost just over 14 percent, considerably less than the other two portfolios but still a surprisingly large loss for such a diversified portfolio.

Not shown in the table is the most conservative 7Twelve Life Stage 70+ Portfolio, which had a return of –9.2 percent in 2008. It is interesting to note that the S&P 500 Index, which is 100 percent stock, had a return of –37.0 percent in 2008 while the Barclays Capital Aggregate Bond Index had a positive return of 5.2 percent. Assuming a balanced blend of 60 percent stocks and 40 percent bonds, the "expected" 60/40 balanced return in 2008 was about –20 percent. With a return of −31.3 percent in 2008 Fidelity Balanced managed to perform well below its "benchmark" expected return.

Considering the performance of all three portfolios over the entire 10-year period, the 7Twelve design provided superior returns with significantly better protection against large losses during 2000, 2001, 2002, and 2008. Moreover, the 7Twelve portfolio (Life Stage 50–60 and Life Stage 60–70) provided an investor with an ending account value that was over $7,000 larger than the Fidelity Freedom 2010 Fund and over $3,600 larger than the Fidelity Balanced Fund.

A significant debate surrounding the design of target date funds is determining what the stated target date represents: Is it the year of investor's retirement *or* death date many years after the stated target date? The answer to this question has a profound impact on the design of the target date fund because it reflects a dramatically different usage of the fund by the investor. Furthermore, if a target date fund is being used as a college funding vehicle, it represents the date that the student enters college. Recognizing that target date funds can be used for several different purposes (or usages) is also vital in achieving appropriate design.

The appropriate time to begin dramatically reducing portfolio risk is within 5 to 10 years of the stated target date, though nearly all existing target date funds fail to do so. I am suggesting that a target date fund that fails to protect the investor's account value as the target date approaches has failed in its primary task.

## 7TWELVE

The appropriate time to begin dramatically reducing portfolio risk is within 5 to 10 years of the stated target date, though nearly all existing target date funds fail to do so.

The performance comparison between Fidelity 2020, Fidelity Balanced, and the 7Twelve portfolio is shown in Table 11.3. The 7Twelve Life Stage portfolios dominated Fidelity 2020 and Fidelity Balanced in both up markets and down markets.

The performance comparisons involving Fidelity 2030 and Fidelity 2040 are presented in Table 11.4 and Table 11.5. Once again, the same pattern is observed: the 7Twelve portfolio provides better performance in nearly all up markets and dramatically better protection during down markets than the largest target date funds in the industry (the Fidelity Freedom Funds) and second largest balanced fund in the mutual fund industry (Fidelity Balanced).

**Table 11.3  Target Retirement Year 2020 (Annual % Returns)**

| Year | Investor Age | Fidelity Freedom 2020 Target Fund (FFFDX) (%) | Fidelity Balanced (FBLAX) (%) | 7Twelve Life Stage Portfolios* (%) |
|---|---|---|---|---|
| 2000 | 45 | −3.03 | 5.32 | 6.78 |
| 2001 | 46 | −9.07 | 2.25 | −1.58 |
| 2002 | 47 | −13.71 | −8.50 | −0.68 |
| 2003 | 48 | 24.90 | 28.24 | 27.08 |
| 2004 | 49 | 9.60 | 10.94 | 17.73 |
| 2005 | 50 | 7.72 | 10.68 | 10.39 |
| 2006 | 51 | 11.61 | 11.65 | 12.82 |
| 2007 | 52 | 8.54 | 8.99 | 10.71 |
| 2008 | 53 | −32.12 | −31.31 | −19.47 |
| 2009 | 54 | 28.86 | 28.05 | 20.94 |
| 3-Year Average Annualized Return | | **−1.72** | **−1.40** | **2.54** |
| 5-Year Average Annualized Return | | **2.68** | **3.45** | **6.07** |
| 10-Year Average Annualized Return | | **1.74** | **5.20** | **7.69** |
| 10-Year Growth of $10,000 | | **$11,889** | **$16,607** | **$20,970** |

*7Twelve Core Portfolio from age 45 to 49; 7Twelve Life Stage 50–60 Portfolio from ages 50 to 54.

**Table 11.4 Retirement Year 2030 (Annual % Returns)**

| Year | Investor Age | Fidelity Freedom 2030 Target Fund (FFFEX) (%) | Fidelity Balanced (FBLAX) (%) | 7Twelve Life Stage Core Portfolio (%) |
|------|------|------|------|------|
| 2000 | 35 | −5.07 | 5.32 | 6.78 |
| 2001 | 36 | −11.69 | 2.25 | −1.58 |
| 2002 | 37 | −17.31 | −8.50 | −0.68 |
| 2003 | 38 | 28.42 | 28.24 | 27.08 |
| 2004 | 39 | 10.45 | 10.94 | 17.73 |
| 2005 | 40 | 8.86 | 10.68 | 12.30 |
| 2006 | 41 | 12.90 | 11.65 | 15.38 |
| 2007 | 42 | 9.27 | 8.99 | 11.25 |
| 2008 | 43 | −36.93 | −31.31 | −24.62 |
| 2009 | 44 | 30.57 | 28.05 | 24.99 |
| 3-Year Average Annualized Return | | **−3.46** | **−1.40** | **1.58** |
| 5-Year Average Annualized Return | | **2.03** | **3.45** | **6.31** |
| 10-Year Average Annualized Return | | **0.84** | **5.20** | **7.81** |
| 10-Year Growth of $10,000 | | **$10,874** | **$16,607** | **$21,212** |

*7Twelve Core Portfolio from age 35 to 44.

# Determining Your Lifecycle Phase

An investor's lifecycle can be segmented into three distinct phases:

1. Accumulation phase prior to retirement (approximately ages 25–55)
2. Transition phase as the investor prepares for retirement (ages 55–65)
3. Distribution phase during the retirement years (over age 65)

**Table 11.5   Retirement Year 2040 (Annual % Returns)**

| Year | Investor Age | Fidelity Freedom 2040 Target Fund (FFFFX) (%) | Fidelity Balanced (FBLAX) (%) | 7Twelve Life Stage Core Portfolio (%) |
|------|------|------|------|------|
| 2000 | 25 | n/a | 5.32 | 6.78 |
| 2001 | 26 | −13.50 | 2.25 | −1.58 |
| 2002 | 27 | −19.66 | −8.50 | −0.68 |
| 2003 | 28 | 31.16 | 28.24 | 27.08 |
| 2004 | 29 | 11.32 | 10.94 | 17.73 |
| 2005 | 30 | 9.06 | 10.68 | 12.30 |
| 2006 | 31 | 13.50 | 11.65 | 15.38 |
| 2007 | 32 | 9.31 | 8.99 | 11.25 |
| 2008 | 33 | −38.80 | −31.31 | −24.62 |
| 2009 | 34 | 31.65 | 28.05 | 24.99 |
| 3-Year Average Annualized Return | | **−4.15** | **−1.40** | **1.58** |
| 5-Year Average Annualized Return | | **1.74** | **3.45** | **6.31** |
| 10-Year Average Annualized Return | | **n/a** | **5.20** | **7.81** |
| 10-Year Growth of $10,000 | | **n/a** | **$16,607** | **$21,212** |

*7Twelve Core Portfolio from age 25–34.

These three phases are shown in Table 11.6. As you can see, over time our goals as an investor shift from growth to preservation. Accordingly, the design of our investment portfolios must change as we move through the lifecycle.

The primary objective during Stage 1 is to grow assets. As a result, the portfolio will consist primarily of equities until the investor is approximately 55 years old. At approximately 55, the target date fund should begin to aggressively protect the assets in the portfolio, while still attempting to achieve prudent growth.

**Table 11.6   The Shift from Growth to Preservation**

| Lifecycle Investment Stage | Investment Phase | Approximate Ages | Primary Goal | Secondary Goal |
|---|---|---|---|---|
| 1 | Accumulation | 25–55 | Growth | Asset protection |
| 2 | Transition | 55–65 | Asset protection | Reasonable growth |
| 3 | Distribution | Over 65 | Asset preservation | Modest growth |

Here is the philosophy behind Stage 2: The target date should represent the year of retirement. When an investor is 63 years old, they only have two years until the target date. The investor should be brought safely to the target date. Once safely at the point of retirement, the individual should engage in a complete financial review and make needed preparations to begin Stage 3. While in this transition phase from Stage 2 to Stage 3 an investor's portfolio should be protected from large losses.

Stage 3 represents an entirely different experience for the individual. This person is no longer investing money but is now withdrawing money from his or her portfolio. As a result, the portfolio needs to be designed differently. As shown in Chapter 7, portfolios are more fragile during retirement years when they are in "distribution" mode. Target date funds are not an appropriate vehicle for Stage 3—at least not the target date funds currently in circulation. Why? Virtually all target date funds are too aggressive in their asset allocation as they approach the stated target date and beyond the target date as well. Very simply, they take too much risk at the wrong times.

A target date fund can feel good about itself (assuming they have feelings) if it has helped an investor prudently grow assets and then has protected those assets in the years leading up to the target date. At the target date, the target date fund

> ## 7TWELVE
>
> Target date funds need to pass the baton to a portfolio that has been specifically designed for the distribution phase.

may need to yield up the assets to a different portfolio that is more appropriately structured to help the investor meet his or her retirement income needs. An analogy is a relay race in which the baton is passed from one runner to the next. Target date funds need to pass the baton to a portfolio that has been specifically designed for the distribution phase. For example, target date funds do not utilize annuity products in their asset allocation model, whereas portfolios specifically designed for the distribution phase are inclined to use annuities.

## Mismatch 101

The makers of nearly all target date funds are inclined to assume that the investor in a target date fund will stay in the fund until death and, based on that assumption, design an asset allocation model (or glide path) that is very aggressive near and at the target date. The investor, on the other hand, assumes that the stated target date actually means something and, as a result, assumes that in the years leading up to the target date the fund will be considerably insulated from dramatic losses. Many investors, in fact, plan to safely arrive at the target and then withdraw the funds and purchase annuities or build a conservative "distribution" portfolio. One product with two very different sets of assumptions. Welcome to Mismatch 101.

Very simply, in the minds of many investors the target date fund is designed to get them to the target date—but perhaps not beyond. The makers of target date funds, of course, are driven by asset (i.e., money) acquisition and retention. A conservative approach that actually reduces risk as the fund nears the target date has not been widely observed among actual target date funds. In fact, many of the largest target date fund families increased their equity allocation in their target date funds in 2006 and 2007—just in time to get hammered in 2008.

The faulty assumption of virtually every existing target date fund is this: They look past the retirement target date and design the portfolio with death as the ultimate target date. This leads to overly aggressive design when investors are close to the stated target date. For example, in the view of nearly all target date funds, a 63-year-old has about 20 years until death. As a result, the portfolio is too aggressive because the designers of the target date fund view it as the solution for every stage of the investor's lifecycle rather than the vehicle that takes them only to the stated target date. An example of "to-the-target" fund design can be found at www.OnTargetIndex.com.

Recall that target date funds can also be used to save for college expenses of a child. If the target date fund looks beyond the stated target year (naively assuming that target date funds are used only by people saving for retirement), the fund will be far too aggressive and could suffer a large loss when the money is needed for tuition. Designing a target date fund under the fallacy that there is a "long time to recover from losses that occur near the target date" clearly does not work when the fund is being used for college funding. There is not a long time to recover from a loss in the fund if the loss occurred one year before the money is needed.

How did target date funds perform in 2008?

As of December 31, 2008, the average return for all 2010 funds was –23.2 percent. As shown in Table 11.7, the largest single 2010 fund (Fidelity Freedom 2010, which holds about half of all 2010 assets) had a one-year return in 2008 of –25.3 percent. The average return of the four largest 2010 funds (collectively holding 87 percent of all 2010 assets) was –25.8 percent. These 2010 funds were within 24 months of

**Table 11.7   2010 Target Funds and Balanced Funds in 2008**

| | Performance in 2008 (%) | Impact of 2008 Performance on $500,000 Account ($) |
|---|---|---|
| **Four Largest 2010 Target Date Funds** | | |
| Fidelity Freedom 2010 | −25.3 | −126,500 |
| T. Rowe Price Retirement 2010 | −26.7 | −133,500 |
| Vanguard Target Retirement 2010 | −20.7 | −103,500 |
| Principal L/T 2010 | −30.3 | −151,500 |
| **Four Largest Balanced Funds** | | |
| American Funds Balanced | −25.7 | −128,500 |
| Fidelity Balanced | −31.3 | −156,500 |
| Fidelity Puritan | −29.2 | −146,000 |
| Dodge & Cox Balanced | −33.6 | −168,000 |
| **7Twelve Life Stage 60-70** | **−14.3** | **−72,000** |
| S&P 500 Index (SPY) | −36.7 | −183,500 |

2010 (the stated target date of the fund) when they experienced these dramatic losses. That is exactly what should *not* happen to a 63-year-old investor who is making plans to retire in the next 18 to 24 months.

Balanced funds (of the "moderate allocation" variety) did not fare any better. Moderate balanced funds have an equity allocation of around 60 percent and a fixed income allocation of about 40 percent, which (unlike a target date fund) does not vary according to the age of the investor. The average performance in 2008 among the 125 moderate allocation balanced funds was a discouraging −26.6 percent. The four largest balanced funds, accounting for nearly half of all the money invested in balanced funds, are shown in the Table 11.7. Their average performance was even worse, at −29.9 percent. By comparison, the 100 percent equity S&P 500 index (using SPY as the investable product) had a return of -36.7 percent. The risk reducing con-cepts of "balanced" and "target date fund glide path" did not shine in 2008 (a sizeable understatement). However, Table 11.7 also includes the performance of the 7Twelve Life Stage 60–70 Portfolio. Whereas the target date funds and balanced funds lost between $125,000 and $170,000 (assuming a starting portfolio value of $500,000 on January 1, 2008), the 7Twelve Life Stage 60–70 Portfolio lost only $72,000 in the meltdown of 2008.

Risk control in portfolios is always important, but it is par-ticularly important during the years just prior to the transition to retirement. The 7Twelve Life Stage portfolios are designed to do exactly that. In the early years of the accumulation phase, growth is paramount. Importantly, the 7Twelve Life Stage portfolios do that too.

In summary, we can see that a multi-asset portfolio recipe (such as the 7Twelve) has demonstrated better overall risk-adjusted performance than the typical balanced fund and the typical target date fund over the past 10 years (using Fidelity products as representative).

How does all this impact your 401(k) account? Using the 7Twelve portfolio blueprint provided in this book, you can select funds in your 401(k) menu to create your own 7Twelve portfolio. You can build a better 401(k) account by assem-bling a more diversified mix of funds. If your 401(k) sponsor (your employer) doesn't provide all the needed funds to cre-ate a 7Twelve portfolio, just do your best with what is available to you. Plus, you can always ask your employer to add certain types of funds that are currently missing in the menu.

In the next chapter, we will address the problem of under-saving. Let's face it—it's not the portfolio's fault if we don't save enough.

# THE PROBLEM OF UNDERSAVING

Before proceeding, I'd like to share a philosophy about investing and preparing for retirement.

There are two engines of growth in an investment portfolio:

1. Contributions from the investor
2. Growth produced by the performance of the investment portfolio

In Chapter 11, I outlined a potential flaw in the design of target date funds *if* they attempt to make up for "undersaving" on the part of the investor. The only way to do that is to expose the investor to more risk. Given what happened in 2008 to target date funds, we know that is not the right approach. So the burden of retirement falls upon the shoulders of each individual—exactly where it should be.

Contributions are largely controllable by the investor, while performance (particularly in the short run) is not. As a result, investors who rely upon the performance of the portfolio to do the "heavy lifting" (that is, to make up for their insufficient contributions) will usually fall into the trap of having

> ## 7TWELVE
>
> Investing is not supposed to be exciting or laced with bravado. It is a long-term, systematic, and rather boring endeavor. (And that's okay!)

too much equity exposure and therefore be exposed to too much risk.

The performance or "return" of an investment portfolio *should* accomplish two primary goals:

1. Preserve and protect the contributions of the investor.
2. Provide a *modest* rate of return.

The performance of a portfolio should not be expected to make up for undersaving on the part of the investor. It is our job as investors to adequately contribute to our investment accounts. A contribution rate of 1 to 2 percent of our income into our 401(k) account or individual retirement account (IRA) is simply inadequate.

In an era of super-sized meals, drinks, vehicles, houses, and egos, the notion of a "modest" rate of return may sound rather unsophisticated. At this point in the book, I will simply invite you to consider that investing is not supposed to be exciting or laced with bravado. It is a long-term, systematic, and rather boring endeavor. Get your excitement elsewhere. A modest return consistently achieved gets the job done—and with less emotional turmoil.

## Chasing Returns Is a Loser's Game

Sadly, many investors view the performance of their investment portfolio as the primary engine of growth rather than their own contributions. With that mind-set, they focus on hot stock tips, tend to jump in and out of the mutual funds based on short-term performance, and select asset allocations that are overly aggressive. There is no investing plan, only erratic emotionally driven buy and sell decisions. Such behavior is commonly referred to as "chasing returns." It's expensive, and it's a loser's game.

Why would otherwise rational individuals develop irrational performance expectations for their retirement portfolios? To this exact point, a 2009 retirement study by T. Rowe Price (*Revisiting T. Rowe Price's Asset Allocation Glide-Path Strategy*) contained the following statement: "[R]elatively few retirees have saved enough . . . because many investors undersave and overspend, they tend to need help from their portfolios[.]"

Disappointing outcomes are likely when investors "need help" from their portfolios. Indeed, the phrase "need help" is a significant understatement. The blunt truth is that far too many investors expect their retirement portfolios to generate heroic performance that will save them from years of under-contributing to their retirement accounts. This misguided hope leads to portfolio allocations that are far too aggressive (as noted in the previous chapter). Indeed, the meltdown in 2008 of millions of retirement accounts held by individuals over the age of 60 is all the evidence we need.

People who have saved adequately throughout their working career don't need an aggressive portfolio when they are over 60 years old. They have already done all the heavy lifting throughout their working careers. At that point, the portfolio's main task is to keep all the contributions safe while providing a modest return.

Consider this sobering fact. As of June 2009, the median balance in a defined contribution plan (such as a 401(k) account) among people 65 years old and older was $56,212 (Employee Benefits Research Institute [EBRI], Issue Brief, No. 333. August 2009). The median is the midpoint. That means that half of all the defined contribution plans in the United States owned by people 65 or older have a balance of less than $56,212. That is staggering. Why are so many retirement account balances so small? The answer (to reiterate the point made by T. Rowe Price's study) is insufficient contributions— which has nothing to do with asset allocation or portfolio performance. It's like trying to drive from San Francisco to Los Angeles on one gallon of gas. It's not possible because the gas tank is "underfunded."

Let me introduce a simplistic, but illustrative, example. A 25-year-old worker begins her career earning $35,000 per year. Her salary increases 3 percent annually over the next 40 years. If she invests *10 percent* of her annual gross salary into a 401(k), she will have $275,000 accumulated by age 65 assuming a rate of return of 0 percent. She has over a quarter of a million dollars entirely as a result of her own contributions— representing the first engine of growth. Now, let's consider the second engine of growth, namely, portfolio performance. If her 401(k) account averages a conservative return of 6 percent per year, her account value at age 65 will be $880,000 (of which $275,000 were her contributions). Clearly the "return" of the portfolio is a significant part of the ending account value, but so are her contributions.

Let's now assume that our 25-year-old worker invests only *2 percent* of her salary each year until she retires at age 65. Assuming a 0 percent return in her retirement portfolio, she will have an account balance of $55,000. Assuming a 6 percent average annualized return over 40 years her balance would only be $176,000. To achieve an ending balance of $880,000 at age 65 (with her low 2 percent contribution rate), her retirement portfolio would need to generate a return of 12.4 percent annually. In other words, her inadequate contributions force the portfolio to do the heavy lifting. Can a portfolio reasonably produce an average annualized return of 12.4 percent over a 40-year period?

To address this question, let's take a look at the performance of several key asset classes since 1926. We will consider the S&P 500 Index (large-cap U.S. stock), U.S. bonds, and a 60/40 balanced mix (60 percent large-cap U.S. stock and 40 percent U.S. bonds).

Shown in the graph below (Figure 12.1) are forty-five 40-year average annualized rolling returns for U.S. large stock, U.S. bonds, and a 60 percent stock/40 percent bonds mix. In other words, each individual square, triangle, or circle represents the performance over a specific 40-year period. The first 40-year period was from 1926 to 1965, the second from 1927 to 1966, and so on.

A 100 percent bond portfolio and a 60 percent stock/40 percent bond portfolio never produced an average annualized return of 12.4 percent over any of the forty-five 40-year periods. In fact, a 100 percent U.S. large-cap stock portfolio only produced the needed return of 12.4 percent (or more) on two occasions (out of forty-five 40-year periods). Of course, a 100 percent stock portfolio will be considerably more volatile

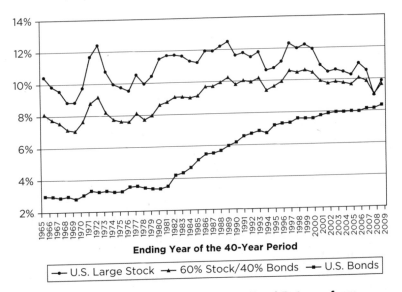

Figure 12.1    45 Forty-Year Rolling Annualized Returns from 1926–2009

than a bond portfolio or 60/40 portfolio, which creates a new set of problems for investors that react badly to short-run gyrations in their retirement accounts.

Since 1926, the average annualized return for large-cap U.S. stock over forty-five 40-year rolling periods has been 10.9 percent, for bonds 5.4 percent, and 9.1 percent for a 60/40 balanced portfolio. Notably, a 60/40 balanced portfolio produced an average annualized return of over 8 percent in thirty-five of the forty-five 40-year rolling periods (or 78 percent of the time).

Let's revisit our 25-year old worker one more time. We will now assume that she invests 6 percent of her $35,000 salary at age 25 (not the ideal target of 10 percent, but an improvement upon the current contribution rate in the United States) and earns a modest return of 8 percent per year over the 40-year period prior to her retirement. If her salary increases 3 percent per year, she will have an account balance of just over $840,000 when she retires at age 65. That is a good outcome.

A contribution rate of 6 percent is achievable as is a long-run portfolio return of 8 percent (as demonstrated by the 60/40 portfolio in Figure 12.1). These are not academic or theoretical possibilities. These are behaviors that real people can achieve. Perhaps it may require sacrifice to save 6 percent of salary. Sacrifice is good for the soul.

## Add Plenty of Patience, Perspective, and Persistence

Patience, perspective, and persistence are the common attributes of successful investors. Unsuccessful investors tend to react to market volatility with impatience, short-sightedness, and a fleeting commitment to their investment plan (if there is a plan at all).

For example, the 40-year rolling returns shown in Figure 12.1 look relatively steady and consistent. Shown in Figure 12.2 are the average annualized returns for large-cap U.S. stock, U.S.

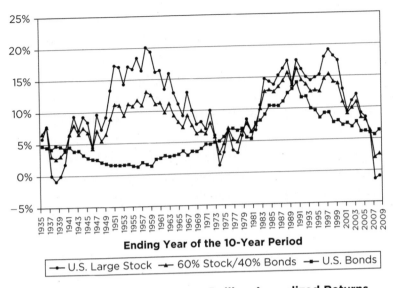

**Ending Year of the 10-Year Period**

-•- U.S. Large Stock  -▲- 60% Stock/40% Bonds  -■- U.S. Bonds

**Figure 12.2   Seventy-Five 10-Year Rolling Annualized Returns from 1926 to 2009**

bonds, and a 60/40 portfolio over much shorter rolling time frames of 10 years. Suddenly things don't look quite so peaceful over the seventy-five rolling 10-year periods since 1926. The triangles in Figure 12.1 and 12.2 represent a simple two-asset balanced 60/40 portfolio, with 60 percent large-cap U.S. stock and 40 percent bonds. The dots represent large-cap U.S. stock, and the squares represent the U.S. bonds.

When the rolling period is shortened, real life volatility is observed . . . and experienced. Patience and perspective will create persistence during periods of unsettling market volatility. (It will also help to have a well-designed multi-asset portfolio!) More than any other single attribute, successful investors are persistent.

## 7TWELVE

More than any other single attribute, successful investors are persistent.

Even though the average 10-year rolling return of a 60/40 portfolio has been 9.07 percent since 1926, it failed to produce a 10-year annualized return of 8 percent in thirty-five of the seventy-five 10-year periods, or nearly half of the time. Again, patience and perspective will generate the needed persistence to endure periods of underperformance (or at least perceived underperformance).

Chapter 13 takes a brief look at what is referred to as the "equity premium." A basic understanding of the equity premium is useful in order to appreciate the common wisdom that governs (for better or worse) the design of most investment portfolios.

# OF STOCKS, BONDS, AND RISK

The term *equity premium* refers to the extra return that investors can expect by allocating more of their portfolios to stocks and less to bonds. Said differently, the equity premium is the return of stocks above and beyond the return of bonds. An investor's acceptance or rejection of the notion of an equity premium will greatly impact how that person builds a portfolio.

## A Tale of Two Time Frames

I suspect you may have noticed something in Figure 12.1 and 12.2, in the previous chapter—the performance of fixed income (bonds) has been steadily increasing over the past 40 years. The average annual returns for these two key asset classes (large-cap U.S. stock and U.S. bonds) are reported in Table 13.1—but with an unusual twist. The returns of these two assets over the 84-year period from 1926–2009 are divided into two time frames: the 44-year period from 1926 to 1969 and the 40-year period from 1970 to 2009. The bond indexes used in this 84-year analysis were U.S. intermediate government bonds from 1926 to 1975 and the Barclay's Capital Aggregate Bond Index from 1976 to 2009.

**Table 13.1  Two Time Frames**

| Average Annualized Return of Individual Assets | 44-Year Period 1926–1969 (%) | 40-Year Period 1970–2009 (%) |
|---|---|---|
| U.S. Large-cap Stock | 9.75 | 9.87 |
| U.S. Bonds | 2.93 | 8.33 |
| Equity "Premium" (Stock Return Minus Bond Return) | 6.82 | 1.54 |

Over the 44-year period from 1926 to 1969, the average annual return of large-cap U.S. stock was 9.75 percent (using the returns of the S&P 500 Index as representative of large-cap U.S. stock). The average annual return for large-cap U.S. stock over the most recent 40-year period from 1970 to 2009 was 9.87 percent. Thus, the return pattern of the S&P 500 Index has been consistent between these two historical time periods despite considerable fluctuations in the rolling 10-year returns of large-cap U.S. stock (as shown in Figure 12.2).

The historical performance of U.S. bonds shows a very different pattern. The 44-year average annual return between 1926 and 1969 was 2.93 percent. However, the average annual return of U.S. bonds over the recent 40-year period was 8.33 percent. A dramatic shift has occurred in the performance of bonds in the U.S. market over the past 40 years.

However, having said that, you will observe in Figure 12.2 that the rolling 10-year return of U.S. bonds peaked in the late 1980s and early 1990s and has been declining since then (as measured over 10-year rolling periods).

Why does the change in fixed income performance matter? It matters because nearly all investment portfolios are designed around the notion of an "equity premium." The equity premium represents the extra return earned by investing in stock compared to bonds. Over the period from 1926 to 1969, there was a substantial equity premium of 6.82 percent (or 682 bps), meaning that it made sense to build investment portfolios that had higher allocations in stocks and lower allocations in bonds, at least for the majority of the investor's pre-retirement accumulation period.

However, over the most recent 40-year period, the performance advantage of stocks over bonds was greatly reduced. The equity premium over the 40-year period from 1970–2009 was 1.54 percent (or 154 bps).

As a result, portfolio design must adjust and take into account a reduced equity premium. This simply boils down to the fact that a portfolio that is primarily composed of large-cap U.S. stock is not justified—at least if you consider the equity premium to be a useful guideline.

Let's take a look at the equity premium in action over the past 40 years (from 1970 to 2009). Recall that in the most recent 40 years, the equity premium has been significantly smaller than the equity premium in the previous 44-year period from 1926 to 1969. A two-asset portfolio is contrasted against the seven-asset portfolio, both of which have already been described in previous chapters.

As shown in Table 13.2, both portfolios start out with a 100 percent allocation to U.S. bonds and have the same average 40-year return of 8.3 percent. With no equity exposure to stocks, there is no exposure to an equity premium.

Next, we allocate 20 percent to "equities." In the two-asset portfolio that represents a 20 percent allocation to the S&P 500 Index. In the seven-asset portfolio that represents a 20 percent allocation to the seven-asset cluster (which includes five equity assets and two fixed income assets). We see that the average return was the same at 8.9 percent. In both portfolios, the return was higher (8.9 percent versus 8.3 percent) indicating than an equity premium was experienced.

**Table 13.2   Diversification Performance Premium: Average Annual Return from 1970 to 2009**

| Allocation to S&P 500/Allocation to U.S. Bonds (%) | Two-Asset Portfolio (%) | Allocation to 7-Assets/ Allocation to U.S. Bonds (%) | Seven-Asset Portfolio (%) |
|---|---|---|---|
| 0/100 | 8.3 | 0/100 | 8.3 |
| 20/80 | 8.9 | 20/80 | 8.9 |
| 40/60 | 9.3 | 40/60 | 9.3 |
| 60/40 | 9.6 | 60/40 | 9.8 |
| 80/20 | 9.8 | 80/20 | 10.1 |
| 100/0 | 9.9 | 100/0 | 10.5 |

Interestingly, as shown in Table 13.3, the worst three-year cumulative percentage return was actually better in the 20/80 allocation compared to the 100 percent bond allocation (i.e., the 0/100 allocation). This was true for both portfolios, but even more pronounced (for the better) in the seven-asset portfolio.

In both portfolios, a 20/80 asset allocation was superior to a 0/100 allocation in both performance and risk. This is a classic phenomenon in which adding stocks to an all-bond portfolio increases return and reduces risk. The question is, at what stock/bond allocation does this phenomenon stop working?

We find the breaking point in the 40/60 allocation. Both portfolios demonstrate an equity premium because the performance is higher than in the 20/80 allocation (9.3 percent in the 40/60 allocation versus 8.9 percent in the 20/80 allocation). However, in both portfolios, the risk increases. In the two-asset portfolio, the worst three-year return was –0.4 percent with a 40/60 allocation compared to 7.9 percent with a 20/80 allocation. Higher return was achieved in the 40/60 two-asset portfolio, but at the expense of experiencing a worse worst-case cumulative three-year percentage return.

**Table 13.3   Diversification Risk Premium (worst 3-year cumulative % return) from 1970 to 2009**

| Allocation to S&P 500/Allocation to U.S. Bonds (%) | Two-Asset Portfolio (%) | Allocation to 7-Assets/Allocation to U.S. Bonds (%) | Seven-Asset Portfolio (%) |
|---|---|---|---|
| 0/100 | 6.2 | 0/100 | 6.2 |
| 20/80 | 7.9 | 20/80 | 11.7 |
| 40/60 | −0.4 | 40/60 | 5.8 |
| 60/40 | −13.4 | 60/40 | −0.3 |
| 80/20 | −26.1 | 80/20 | −6.7 |
| 100/0 | −37.6 | 100/0 | −13.3 |

In the seven-asset portfolio, the increased return with a 40/60 allocation (9.3 percent versus 8.9 percent in the 20/80 allocation) was associated with a slight reduction in worst-case three-year return from positive 11.7 percent in the 20/80 allocation to positive 5.8 percent in the 40/60 allocation. Obviously, a positive worst-case three-year return is good in either case. A broadly diversified portfolio produces a better risk–return trade-off than a two-asset portfolio.

The ubiquitous 60/40 portfolio is next. Here we see the seven-asset portfolio nudge ahead of the two-asset portfolio in terms of raw return (9.8 percent in the seven-asset portfolio versus 9.6 percent in the two-asset portfolio). Nevertheless, both portfolios demonstrated an equity premium by producing a higher return in the 60/40 allocation compared to the 40/60 allocation. Importantly, the equity premium was slightly larger in the seven-asset portfolio, suggesting that the seven-asset portfolio has ingredients that are capturing aspects of the "equity" premium that a sole equity investment into the S&P 500 Index is not.

The next allocation is 80 percent stock/20 percent bonds (or in the case of the seven-asset portfolio, 80 percent seven-asset portfolio/20 percent bonds). As a reminder, two of the seven assets are fixed income (bonds and cash), meaning that 1/7 of the 80 percent equity allocation in the seven-asset portfolio is in bonds and another 1/7 is in cash. The net result is that the 80/20 allocation in the seven-asset portfolio actually results in a bond allocation of more than 20 percent (31.4 percent to be exact).

This is very important to realize because the 80/20 seven-asset portfolio has a 30-basis-point higher return than the 80/20 two-asset portfolio—despite having a bond allocation that is 50 percent larger than the two-asset portfolio (as well as a cash allocation of 11.4 percent). This represents more than an equity premium. What we are seeing now is what I will call a diversification premium. The seven-asset portfolio has it, but the two-asset portfolio doesn't.

As shown in Table 13.3, the risk in the 80/20 seven-asset portfolio is a fraction of the risk in the two-asset portfolio: −26.1 percent worst three-year cumulative percentage return for the two-asset portfolio versus −6.7 percent for the seven-asset portfolio. This is also a manifestation of the diversification premium. The diversification premium includes the equity premium but is more than the equity premium. The only way to "extract" the equity premium is to build a diversified portfolio such as the 7Twelve. In doing so, you will harvest a diversification premium.

The last asset allocation model is 100/0, meaning 100 percent S&P 500 allocation in the two-asset portfolio and 100 percent allocation to the seven-asset model with no additional allocation

---

### 7TWELVE

The only way to extract the equity "premium" is to build a diversified portfolio such as the 7Twelve. In doing so, you will harvest a diversification premium.

to bonds. A very intriguing result occurs. The return of the two-asset portfolio increases only slightly, from 9.8 percent to 9.9 percent. In other words, there was virtually no equity premium in the two-asset portfolio when moving from an 80 percent allocation to a 100 percent allocation in the S&P 500 Index.

In large part, this is due to the strong return of bonds during the past 40 years and the large losses experienced by large-cap U.S. stock in four of the past 10 years. The bottom line is this: Over the 40-year period from 1970 to 2009, there was essentially no advantage in building a 100 percent stock portfolio because the return in an 80/20 portfolio was basically equivalent.

In fact, a 100 percent stock portfolio had a worst-case three-year return of –37.6 percent without providing a sufficiently larger return to compensate for the increased risk. More risk with basically the same return indicates that there was no more equity premium to be had after an 80 percent allocation to stock (in a two-asset portfolio).

In the seven-asset portfolio, there was still an equity premium to be achieved by moving from an 80 percent allocation to a 100 percent allocation. The return increased from 10.1 percent to 10.5 percent, or an increase in 40 basis points. The "equity" premium doesn't disappear in a diversified portfolio because diversification produces its own premium—which looks and acts like an equity premium. In addition, a diversified portfolio generated higher returns at the high equity allocation levels compared to the two-asset portfolio.

We have observed that a diversified portfolio keeps the equity premium alive at the higher equity allocations of 80/20 and 100/0, whereas the equity premium is nearly fully extracted at the 80/20 allocation in a two-asset portfolio. Whether or not this will be the case going forward is unknown, but that is the way things played out over the past 40 years.

As shown in Table 13.3, the seven-asset portfolio has substantially less downside risk than the two-asset portfolio at the higher allocation levels (60/40, 80/20, and 100/0). This is a huge benefit, and it is obtained only through broad diversification.

Remember that the 100/0 allocation in the seven-asset portfolio was actually 72 percent spread equally among five equity funds (large-cap U.S. stock, small-cap U.S. stock, non–U.S. stock, real estate, commodities) and 28 percent spread equally among two fixed income funds (U.S. bonds and cash). So we now can see that a 72 percent equity allocation can out-perform a 100 percent equity allocation as long as the 72 percent is diversified.

We also can see that including bonds in a portfolio has not dramatically lowered portfolio performance over the past 40 years. A 100 percent bond portfolio generated a 40-year average return of 8.3 percent whereas a 100 percent stock portfolio produced a 40-year return of 9.9 percent—that's not a huge difference when you also consider that the worst 3-year cumulative return in an all-bond portfolio was a positive 6.2 percent compared to –37.6 percent in the all-stock portfolio.

## The "Diversification" Premium

The 7Twelve portfolio uses twelve funds, not seven. The seven-asset portfolio was used in this chapter because I wanted to study the diversification premium over the longest possible time frame, in this case 40 years. Some of the funds in the 7Twelve portfolio don't have a 40-year history.

Lest you think the 7Twelve portfolio fails to produce the coveted diversification premium, consider the comparison of a two-asset portfolio versus the 7Twelve portfolio over the past 10 years. The various allocations involving the 7Twelve portfolio work like the seven-asset portfolio. For example, the 20/80 allocation indicates a 20 percent allocation to the 7Twelve portfolio and an 80 percent separate allocation to bonds. The performance results in Table 13.4 assume annual rebalancing.

The 7Twelve portfolio generates significantly better returns than a two-asset portfolio at every allocation above 0/100 with dramatically better downside protection. For example, at the 60/40 allocation level, the two-asset portfolio had a 10-year return of 2.6 percent compared to 7.5 percent for the 7Twelve portfolio. The two-asset portfolio had a three-year period in which it lost a cumulative total of 13.4 percent. The worst three-year period for the 7Twelve portfolio produced a cumulative positive return of 7.6 percent. Better return with dramatically less downside risk is what the 7Twelve portfolio delivers

A reminder about average annualized percentage return versus cumulative percentage return (from the discussion in Chapter 3). Average annualized is a "per year" measure, whereas cumulative percentage return is a total start-to-finish measure of performance. For example, if an investment increased from $100 to $200 in five years it had a cumulative percentage return of 100 percent. However, its average annualized return was 14.87 percent. Two different measures of the same event.

In the case of the 0/100 portfolio in Table 13.4, a 10.9 percent worst case 3-year *cumulative* return translates to a 3.51 percent *average annualized* worst-case 3-year return. Obviously, a worst 3-year return that is positive (whether measured in cumulative terms or as an average annualized figure) is a wonderful thing! Likewise, for the 0/100 portfolio a 6.3 percent 10-year average annualized return translates into a 10-year cumulative percentage return of 84.2 percent.

The equity premium is alive and well but achieving it requires the use of various equity and equity-like asset classes. In other words, if you want to harvest a full equity premium, you need to assemble a diversified equity portfolio. Attempting to obtain an equity premium by simply investing in large-cap U.S. stock won't work going forward. Obtaining the equity premium demands diversified equity investments. In essence, the equity premium is derived through the diversification premium.

The old school "meat and potatoes" approach of simply combining large-cap U.S. stock and bonds in the classic 60/40 allocation is inadequate. There's a new menu in town that calls for the use of large-cap U.S. stock, midcap U.S. stock, small-cap U.S. stock, developed non–U.S. stock, emerging non–U.S. stock, real estate, resources, and commodities in the "equities" portion of the portfolio.

Plus, the bond portion of the portfolio also needs to be diversified. Simply using U.S. bonds is not good enough. A diversified

---

### 7TWELVE

If you want to harvest a full equity premium, you'll need to assemble a diversified equity portfolio . . . Simply investing in large-cap U.S. stock won't get it done.

---

**Table 13.4  Diversification Premium in the 7Twelve Portfolio from 2000 to 2009**

| Asset Allocation Model (Equity/Bond) (%) | 10-Year Average Annualized Return (%) | | Worst 3-Year Cumulative Return (%) | |
|---|---|---|---|---|
| | Two-Asset Portfolio | 7Twelve Portfolio | Two-Asset Portfolio | 7Twelve Portfolio |
| 0/100 | 6.3 | 6.3 | 10.9 | 10.9 |
| 20/80 | 5.2 | 6.8 | 12.8 | 16.7 |
| 40/60 | 4.0 | 7.2 | 0.7 | 12.4 |
| 60/40 | 2.6 | 7.5 | −13.4 | 7.6 |
| 80/20 | 0.9 | 7.7 | −26.1 | 2.4 |
| 100/0 | −1.0 | 7.8 | −37.6 | −3.2 |

bond portfolio requires the inclusion of U.S. bonds, inflation protected bonds, non–U.S. bonds, and cash. Permit me to show again my favorite graphic, first introduced way back in Chapter 1. Figure 13.1 shows that a diversified portfolio needs to look like a sliced pizza.

In conclusion, to diversify salsa, you don't add more tomatoes because tomatoes represent the core ingredient. Likewise, in most portfolios (during the accumulation years) the core ingredient is U.S. stock mutual funds. The 7Twelve includes three U.S. stock funds—the most funds in any of the seven asset categories. But to achieve overall portfolio diversification, we don't want to add more U.S. stock funds. That's why we add non–U.S. stock funds (developed and emerging), a real estate fund, a resources fund, and a commodities fund. The 7Twelve portfolio also spices up the fixed income portion of the portfolio with four different bond funds.

The 7Twelve portfolio produces the elusive equity premium precisely because it contains a rich array of ingredients.

The next chapter is the 7Twelve menu itself. Let's make some salsa!

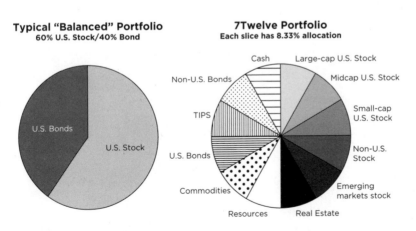

**Figure 13.1 Old School Diversification versus New Age Diversification**

C H A P T E R

# ASSEMBLING YOUR PORTFOLIO

It's time to build it. Put on an apron, we're gonna make some salsa.

As you know, 12 ingredients are needed. I'll provide a short list of funds that can be used in each of the 12 slots in the 7Twelve portfolio. For those who want additional information about prebuilt 7Twelve portfolios, please visit www.7TwelvePortfolio.com.

On the same website, you'll also find software that allows you to compare the performance of mutual funds you may already own against the 7Twelve portfolio over a variety of different time periods.

The performance of the 7Twelve portfolio has been illustrated many times throughout the book, but I'll repeat one more table here. The performance of the 7Twelve portfolio is shown in the far-right column, which represents the average of the performance of all 12 funds (in this case, eleven exchange-traded funds and one money market fund) that were used in building the 7Twelve portfolio.

You can build the 7Twelve portfolio with a large variety of mutual funds and ETFs. Which funds you select as you build your version of the 7Twelve portfolio is entirely up to you.

To help you get started, I have provided a short list of funds within each of the 12 categories in Tables 14.3 through 14.14.

Some of the funds in Table 14.1 don't have a full 10-year history. This may cause you to wonder how I can show a 10-year performance history for all 12 fund categories in Table 14.1. The solution is very straightforward. The performance figures in Table 14.1 represent the returns of actual ETFs. If a particular ETF didn't have a full 10-year history, I used the performance of the index that the ETF mimics—minus the expense ratio of the actual ETF—to fill in the missing returns needed to produce the 10-year performance history reported in Table 14.1 (and in a number of performance tables throughout the book). The underlying indexes behind the 11 ETFs are shown in Table 14.2. The three-month Treasury bill is a proxy for money market fund returns, but it does not represent an underlying index for the money market fund.

This technique produces a very reliable proxy performance history. Recall that ETFs are, by definition, index funds. All ETFs mimic a selected index, so the underlying index represents the return of the actual ETF, minus the expense ratio of the operational ETF. In some cases, the ETF selected had a 10-year history so the proxy technique was not needed.

If you choose to build the 7Twelve portfolio using actively managed funds the performance can, and will, be different from the ETF-based performance in Table 14.1. This doesn't mean you should not build an "active" 7Twelve; it simply means that it will have performance characteristics that are different from an ETF-based (i.e., index-based) 7Twelve. The performance differences between the active and passive 7Twelve portfolios were illustrated in Chapter 10.

The first ingredient in the 7Twelve portfolio is a large-cap U.S. stock fund. Table 14.3 outlines several large-cap U.S. stock mutual funds (MF) and exchange-traded funds (ETF) that could be used. Midcap U.S. stock funds (mutual funds and ETFs)

**Table 14.1  The 7Twelve Portfolio from 2000 to 2009 Using ETF Performance Data (Annual % Returns)**

| Year | Large-cap U.S. Stock (%) | Midcap U.S. Stock (%) | Small-cap U.S. Stock (%) | Non-U.S. Stock (%) | Emerging Non-U.S. Stock (%) | Real Estate (%) | Resources (%) | Commodities (%) | U.S. Bonds (%) | TIPS (%) | International Bonds (%) | Cash (%) | 7Twelve Portfolio (%) |
|---|---|---|---|---|---|---|---|---|---|---|---|---|---|
| 2000 | −9.70 | 17.38 | 21.88 | −14.46 | −27.45 | 26.46 | 15.24 | 24.43 | 11.49 | 12.95 | −3.13 | 6.29 | **6.78** |
| 2001 | −11.86 | −0.90 | 13.70 | −21.71 | −2.73 | 12.45 | −16.00 | −8.68 | 8.31 | 7.68 | −3.41 | 4.16 | **−1.58** |
| 2002 | −21.50 | −14.51 | −14.20 | −15.43 | −7.29 | 3.85 | −13.49 | 24.56 | 10.12 | 16.33 | 21.80 | 1.65 | **−0.68** |
| 2003 | 28.16 | 35.26 | 37.19 | 39.71 | 57.88 | 35.77 | 33.37 | 25.84 | 3.98 | 8.18 | 18.78 | 0.90 | **27.08** |
| 2004 | 10.69 | 15.89 | 23.55 | 18.94 | 26.31 | 30.87 | 24.38 | 37.15 | 4.21 | 8.29 | 11.41 | 1.11 | **17.73** |
| 2005 | 4.86 | 12.51 | 6.18 | 13.35 | 32.25 | 11.99 | 35.96 | 30.87 | 2.31 | 2.52 | −8.18 | 3.01 | **12.30** |
| 2006 | 15.80 | 9.96 | 19.38 | 25.79 | 29.20 | 35.05 | 16.40 | 16.02 | 4.21 | 0.29 | 7.55 | 4.88 | **15.38** |
| 2007 | 5.12 | 7.20 | −6.94 | 9.94 | 37.32 | −16.51 | 33.45 | 31.50 | 6.84 | 11.93 | 10.06 | 5.14 | **11.25** |
| 2008 | −36.70 | −36.39 | −32.19 | −41.01 | −52.46 | −36.91 | −42.88 | −31.73 | 8.41 | −0.53 | 4.22 | 2.77 | **−24.62** |
| 2009 | 26.32 | 37.52 | 30.93 | 26.88 | 76.32 | 30.11 | 37.11 | 16.18 | 3.57 | 8.96 | 5.43 | 0.53 | **24.99** |
| 10-Year Average Annualized Return | −1.00 | 6.10 | 7.76 | 1.00 | 9.88 | 10.52 | 8.67 | 14.49 | 6.30 | 7.53 | 6.06 | 3.03 | **7.81** |
| 10-Year Standard Deviation of Return | 20.90 | 21.97 | 21.78 | 25.87 | 39.23 | 24.14 | 27.38 | 21.17 | 3.12 | 5.49 | 9.64 | 2.01 | **15.11** |
| 10-Year Growth of $10,000 | $9,047 | $18,083 | $21,106 | $11,041 | $25,657 | $27,198 | $22,975 | $38,683 | $18,430 | $20,674 | $18,011 | $13,474 | **$21,212** |

*Note:* Annual returns in this table reflect the performance of actual ETFs that comprise the 7Twelve "Passive" portfolio with annual rebalancing.

**Table 14.2 Underlying Raw Indexes of the 7Twelve Portfolio Mutual Funds and ETFs**

| Mutual Fund or ETF | Underlying Index |
|---|---|
| Large-cap U.S. Stock | S&P 500 Index |
| Midcap U.S. Stock | S&P Midcap 400 Index |
| Small-cap U.S. Value stock | Russell 2000 Value Index |
| Non–U.S. Developed stock | MSCI EAFE Index |
| Non–U.S. Emerging stock | MSCI Emerging Markets Index |
| Real Estate | Dow Jones U.S. Select REIT Index |
| Natural Resources | Goldman Sachs Natural Resources Index |
| Commodities | Deutsche Bank Liquid Commodity Index |
| U.S. Bonds | Barclays Capital Aggregate Bond Index |
| Inflation Protected Bonds | Barclays Capital U.S. Treasury Inflation Note Index |
| Non–U.S. Bonds | Citibank WGBI Non–U.S. Dollar Index |
| Cash | 3-Month Treasury Bill |

are listed in Table 14.4, with small-cap U.S. stock funds in Table 14.5. All of the small-cap stock funds and ETFs have a value-tilt (as discussed in Chapter 9).

Table 14.6 lists developed non–U.S. stock funds, with emerging non–U.S. stock funds in Table 14.7. Real estate funds are highlighted in Table 14.8. Natural resources funds are in Table 14.9, and commodity funds (including two exchange-traded notes) are listed in Table 14.10. Exchange-traded notes are similar to ETFs but they do expose the investor to default risk of the issuer of the note. That is a concern after watching a company like Lehman Brothers slip into the ocean.

Table 14.11 lists several U.S. bond funds, while Table 14.12 highlights five Treasury inflation protected bond funds. Finally, non–U.S. bond funds that made the short-list are in Table 14.13 and two money market (or cash) funds are listed in Table 14.14. There are hundreds of money market funds, so you have vast choices in that category. I chose to list only two very well-known money market funds.

You will notice in the following tables of 7Twelve "ingredients" that ETFs do not have a minimum initial purchase requirement. This is because ETFs are purchased like individual stocks through a broker. So while there is no minimum there will be a commission when you buy and sell ETFs. The vast majority of the funds listed in Tables 14.3 through 14.14 are low-cost index funds. By low-cost, I mean that they have low expense ratios. The expense ratio data is as of December 31, 2009.

To build your own 7Twelve portfolio, you'll want to select one fund from each table. If you want to build a tax-efficient 7Twelve portfolio choose mutual funds that emphasize tax efficiency. For example, Vanguard has a number of mutual funds that are designed to be more tax efficient. There are several 7Twelve mutual funds that have already been assembled. Go to www.7TwelvePortfolio.com to learn more about pre-built 7Twelve portfolios that you can invest in. The website also has monthly performance updates for the 7Twelve portfolios that I've assembled.

One more chapter to go! Once you've built your portfolio, it's time to move on to Chapter 15, which reviews the 7Twelve portfolio investment plan.

**Table 14.3   Large-Cap U.S. Stock Funds**

| Fund Name | Ticker | Type of Fund | Minimum Initial Purchase Req. ($) | Annual Expense Ratio (%) |
|---|---|---|---|---|
| Schwab S&P 500 Index Select | SWPPX | MF | 100 | 0.09 |
| SPDRs | SPY | ETF | — | 0.09 |
| iShares S&P 500 Index | IVV | ETF | — | 0.09 |
| iShares Russell 1000 Index | IWB | ETF | — | 0.15 |
| Vanguard 500 Index Investor | VFINX | MF | 3,000 | 0.18 |

### Table 14.4  Midcap U.S. Stock Funds

| Fund Name | Ticker | Type of Fund | Minimum Initial Purchase Req. ($) | Annual Expense Ratio (%) |
|---|---|---|---|---|
| Vanguard Mid Cap ETF | VO | ETF | — | 0.15 |
| iShares S&P MidCap 400 Index | IJH | ETF | — | 0.21 |
| iShares Russell Midcap Index | IWR | ETF | — | 0.21 |
| MidCap SPDRs | MDY | ETF | — | 0.25 |
| Vanguard Mid Cap Index | VIMSX | MF | 3,000 | 0.27 |

### Table 14.5  Small-Cap Value Funds

| Fund Name | Ticker | Type of Fund | Minimum Initial Purchase Req. ($) | Annual Expense Ratio (%) |
|---|---|---|---|---|
| Vanguard Small Cap Value ETF | VBR | ETF | — | 0.15 |
| iShares S&P SmallCap 600 Value Index | IJS | ETF | — | 0.25 |
| Vanguard Small Cap Value Index | VISVX | MF | 3,000 | 0.28 |
| iShares Morningstar Small Value Index | JKL | ETF | — | 0.30 |
| iShares Russell 2000 Value Index | IWN | ETF | — | 0.33 |

### Table 14.6  Developed Non–U.S. Stock Funds

| Fund Name | Ticker | Type of Fund | Minimum Initial Purchase Req. ($) | Annual Expense Ratio (%) |
|---|---|---|---|---|
| Schwab International Index | SWISX | MF | 100 | 0.19 |
| Vanguard FTSE All-World ex-U.S. ETF | VEU | ETF | — | 0.25 |
| Vanguard Developed Markets Index | VDMIX | MF | 3,000 | 0.29 |
| iShares MSCI EAFE Index | EFA | ETF | — | 0.35 |

### Table 14.7   Emerging Non–U.S. Stock Funds

| Fund Name | Ticker | Type of Fund | Minimum Initial Purchase Req. ($) | Annual Expense Ratio (%) |
|---|---|---|---|---|
| Vanguard Emerging Markets Stock ETF | VWO | ETF | — | 0.27 |
| Vanguard Emerging Markets Stock Index | VEIEX | MF | 3,000 | 0.39 |
| SPDR S&P Emerging Markets | GMM | ETF | — | 0.59 |
| iShares MSCI Emerging Markets Index | EEM | ETF | — | 0.72 |

### Table 14.8   Real Estate Funds

| Fund Name | Ticker | Type of Fund | Minimum Initial Purchase Req. ($) | Annual Expense Ratio(%) |
|---|---|---|---|---|
| Vanguard REIT Index ETF | VNQ | ETF | — | 0.15 |
| SPDR Dow Jones REIT | RWR | ETF | — | 0.25 |
| Vanguard REIT Index | VGSIX | MF | 3,000 | 0.26 |
| iShares Cohen & Steers Realty Majors | ICF | ETF | — | 0.35 |
| T. Rowe Price Real Estate | TRREX | MF | 2,500 | 0.75 |

### Table 14.9   Natural Resources Funds

| Fund Name | Ticker | Type of Fund | Minimum Initial Purchase Req. ($) | Annual Expense Ratio (%) |
|---|---|---|---|---|
| Materials Select Sector SPDR | XLB | ETF | — | 0.21 |
| Vanguard Materials ETF | VAW | ETF | — | 0.25 |
| iShares S&P North American Natural Resources | IGE | ETF | — | 0.48 |
| T. Rowe Price New Era | PRNEX | MF | 2,500 | 0.66 |
| Fidelity Select Natural Resources | FNARX | MF | 2,500 | 0.85 |

## Table 14.10 Commodity Funds

| Fund Name | Ticker | Type of Fund | Minimum Initial Purchase Req. ($) | Annual Expense Ratio (%) |
|---|---|---|---|---|
| iShares S&P GSCI Commodity-Indexed Trust | GSG | ETF | — | 0.75 |
| iPath Dow Jones-AIG Commodity Idx TR ETN | DJP | ETN* | — | 0.75 |
| ELEMENTS Rogers Intl Commodity ETN | RJI | ETN* | — | 0.75 |
| PowerShares DB Commodity Index Tracking | DBC | ETF | — | 0.83 |

*ETN stands for exchange-traded note. A note has advantages and disadvantages compared to an exchange-traded fund. The primary disadvantage is that it is exposed to default risk of the issuer of the note.

## Table 14.11 U.S. Bond Funds

| Fund Name | Ticker | Type of Fund | Minimum Initial Purchase Req. ($) | Annual Expense Ratio (%) |
|---|---|---|---|---|
| SPDR Barclays Capital Aggregate Bond | LAG | ETF | — | 0.13 |
| Vanguard Intermediate Term Bond ETF | BIV | ETF | — | 0.14 |
| Vanguard Total Bond Market ETF | BND | ETF | — | 0.14 |
| Vanguard Intermediate Term Bond Index | VBIIX | MF | 3,000 | 0.22 |
| Vanguard Total Bond Market Index | VBMFX | MF | 3,000 | 0.22 |
| iShares Barclays Aggregate Bond | AGG | ETF | — | 0.24 |

**Table 14.12   Treasury Inflation-Protected Bond Funds**

| Fund Name | Ticker | Type of Fund | Minimum Initial Purchase Req. ($) | Annual Expense Ratio (%) |
|---|---|---|---|---|
| SPDR Barclays Capital TIPS | IPE | ETF | — | 0.18 |
| iShares Barclays TIPS Bond | TIP | ETF | — | 0.20 |
| Vanguard Inflation-Protected Securities | VIPSX | MF | 3,000 | 0.25 |
| American Century Inflation-Adjusted Bond | ACITX | MF | 2,500 | 0.49 |
| T. Rowe Price Inflation-Protected Bond | PRIPX | MF | 2,500 | 0.50 |

**Table 14.13   International Bond Funds**

| Fund Name | Ticker | Type of Fund | Minimum Initial Purchase Req. ($) | Annual Expense Ratio (%) |
|---|---|---|---|---|
| iShares S&P/Citi International Treasury Bond | IGOV | ETF | — | 0.35 |
| SPDR Barclays Capital International Treasury Bond | BWX | ETF | — | 0.50 |
| T. Rowe Price International Bond | RPIBX | MF | 2,500 | 0.81 |
| American Century International Bond | BEGBX | MF | 2,500 | 0.83 |

**Table 14.14   Cash Funds (i.e., money market funds)**

| Fund Name | Ticker | Type of Fund | Minimum Initial Purchase Req. ($) | Annual Expense Ratio (%) |
|---|---|---|---|---|
| Vanguard Prime Money Market | VMMXX | MM | 3,000 | 0.25 |
| Fidelity Select Money Market | FSLXX | MM | 2,500 | 0.33 |

CHAPTER

# 3 SECRETS + 4 PRINCIPLES = 7TWELVE PERFECTION

The data have spoken. Diversification is the only logical approach to building durable portfolios for the preretirement accumulation years as well as the postretirement distribution phase.

The 7Twelve portfolio represents a starting point for every investor. It is the diversified "core" element that represents the first building block in a portfolio. Based on the needs of each individual investor, a variety of different assets can be added around the "core."

Let me suggest a plan that covers the entire lifecycle of an investor. Clearly, it is only a general guideline. Individual adaptations are expected based on your own individual and unique circumstances. But it's easier to adapt if you first have a plan. The plan is outlined in Table 15.1. You'll recognize it from Chapter 7. I believe in repetition.

The important thing to consider when you look at the four different life-stage asset allocation models is that the percentages are not set in stone. Table 15.1 is mathematically precise in terms of all the allocations. It's the plan for engineers and other people that really dig precision—geeks like me.

**Table 15.1  The 7Twelve Investment Plan for Engineers (and other detail-oriented folks)**

| Life Stage Portfolio → (based on "Allocation Age") | Core 7Twelve Model | 7Twelve Life Stage 50-60 | 7Twelve Life Stage 60-70 | 7Twelve Life Stage 70+ |
|---|---|---|---|---|
| Approximate Asset Allocation Model (% Equity/% Fixed Income) | 65/35 | 50/50 | 40/60 | 25/75 |
| Generally appropriate for . . . | Investors in the age range of 20-50 | Investors in the age range of 50-60 | Investors in the age range of 60-70 | Investors in the age range of 70+ |
| Investment Objective | Early accumulation years. Preretirement | Late accumulation years. Preretirement | Early distribution period. Postretirement | Late distribution period. Postretirement |

**7Twelve Life Stage Asset Allocation Model**

| 7Twelve Mutual Funds | Allocation to Each Equity Mutual Fund | | | |
|---|---|---|---|---|
| Large-cap U.S. Stock (%) | 8.33 % | 6.67% | 5.0% | 3.33% |
| Midcap U.S. Stock (%) | 8.33% | 6.67% | 5.0% | 3.33% |
| Small-cap U.S. Stock (%) | 8.33% | 6.67% | 5.0% | 3.33% |
| Non-U.S. Stock (%) | 8.33% | 6.67% | 5.0% | 3.33% |
| Emerging Markets (%) | 8.33% | 6.67% | 5.0% | 3.33% |
| Real Estate (%) | 8.33% | 6.67% | 5.0% | 3.33% |
| Natural Resources (%) | 8.33% | 6.67% | 5.0% | 3.33% |
| Commodities (%) | 8.33% | 6.67% | 5.0% | 3.33% |
| | Allocation to Each Fixed Income Mutual Fund | | | |
| U.S. Bonds | 8.33% | 6.67% | 5.0% | 3.33% |
| International Bonds | 8.33% | 6.67% | 5.0% | 3.33% |
| TIPS (Inflation Protected Bonds) | 8.33% | 16.67% | 25.0% | 33.33% |
| Cash | 8.33% | 16.67% | 25.0% | 33.33% |

**Table 15.2  The 7Twelve Investment Plan for Artists and Poets**

| Life Stage Portfolio → (based on "Allocation Age") | Core 7Twelve Model | 7Twelve Life Stage 50–60 | 7Twelve Life Stage 60–70 | 7Twelve Life Stage 70+ |
|---|---|---|---|---|
| **Approximate Asset Allocation Model (% Equity/% Fixed Income)** | **65/35** | **50/50** | **40/60** | **25/75** |
| Generally appropriate for . . . | Investors in the age range of 20–50 | Investors in the age range of 50–60 | Investors in the age range of 60–70 | Investors in the age range of 70+ |
| Investment Objective | Early accumulation years. Preretirement | Late accumulation years. Preretirement | Early distribution period. Postretirement | Late distribution period. Postretirement |

**7Twelve Life Stage Asset Allocation Model**

**7Twelve Mutual Funds**

| | | Allocation to Each Equity Mutual Fund | | |
|---|---|---|---|---|
| Large-cap U.S. Stock | 8% | 6% | 5% | 3% |
| Midcap U.S. Stock | 8% | 6% | 5% | 3% |
| Small-cap U.S. Stock | 8% | 6% | 5% | 3% |
| Non–U.S. Stock | 8% | 6% | 5% | 3% |
| Emerging Markets | 8% | 6% | 5% | 3% |
| Real Estate | 8% | 6% | 5% | 3% |
| Natural Resources | 8% | 6% | 5% | 3% |
| Commodities | 8% | 6% | 5% | 3% |
| | | Allocation to Each Fixed Income Mutual Fund | | |
| U.S. Bonds | 9% | 7% | 5% | 3% |
| International Bonds | 9% | 7% | 5% | 3% |
| TIPS (Inflation Protected Bonds) | 9% | 19% | 25% | 35% |
| Cash | 9% | 19% | 25% | 35% |

Table 15.2 is the same stuff, but not quite so nitpicky. The percentages have been rounded.

Here's the important thing: They will both behave nearly identically. You see, precision is not the secret. The secret to investing is actually three secrets:

1. *First secret.* Successful investing requires patience that is measured in years, not weeks.
2. *Second secret.* Successful investing is boring. If you want thrills, ride a bike in a big city.
3. *Third secret.* Successful investing requires diversification depth and breadth.

---

### FOUR PRINCIPLES OF THE 7TWELVE PORTFOLIO

1. Don't overmanage your investments. Check your accounts quarterly. More often than that is too often. The 7Twelve website (www.7TwelvePortfolio.com) has performance updates for the 7Twelve portfolios that I've assembled.
2. Expect ups and downs. Don't react to either. Let rebalancing do the reacting for you.
3. Enjoy your life. Enjoy your family. Spend time doing the things you truly value. Festering over your portfolio will only distract you from more important things.
4. Consider the lesson learned by Joseph (you know, the fella with the amazing technicolor dreamcoat) in Egypt so many years ago: Build up a reserve in the good years to prepare for the lean years. (As I recall, the number 7 factored in to that situation as well.) In other words, always have a "rainy day" reserve fund. When markets go against you and your portfolio has been hurt, withdraw needed funds from your reserve fund (such as a money market fund or a savings account). *At retirement, having a reserve fund equal to one or two years' worth of annual income is a great goal.*

This book has been primarily focused on the third secret. I've given you my best shot with respect to diversification depth and breadth. You're on your own with the first two secrets. But I can offer some advice. After you've built the 7Twelve portfolio (or had a financial advisor build it for you), focus on the four principles on the previous page.

Well mate, that's the 7Twelve portfolio and the 7Twelve "Life Stage" investment plan to help you assemble an age-appropriate diversified investment portfolio at each major phase in the lifecycle.

Next on your reading list . . . something about rocket science perhaps. Or maybe a good cookbook.

# ABOUT THE AUTHOR

Craig L. Israelsen, Ph.D., was born and raised in northern California. He is currently an Associate Professor at Brigham Young University in Provo, Utah, where he teaches personal and family finance to more than 1,200 students each year.

He holds a Ph.D. in Family Resource Management from Brigham Young University. He received a B.S. in Agribusiness and a M.S. in Agricultural Economics from Utah State University.

Prior to teaching at BYU, he was on the faculty of the University of Missouri–Columbia for 14 years where he taught personal and family finance in the Personal Financial Planning Department.

Primary among his research interests is the analysis of mutual funds and the design of investment portfolios. He writes monthly for *Financial Planning* magazine and is a regular contributor to the *Journal of Indexes* and *Horsesmouth .com*. His research has also been published in the *Journal of Financial Planning, Journal of Asset Management* (U.K.), *Journal of Performance Measurement, Asia Financial Planning Journal* (Singapore), *Journal of Family and Economic Issues*, and *Financial Counseling and Planning.*

His research has been cited in *Fortune, Christian Science Monitor, Wall Street Journal, Newsweek, Forbes, Smart Money Magazine, Kiplinger Retirement Report, Advisor Perspective, Dow Jones Market Watch, Family Circle*, and *Bottom Line Personal.*

He and Phil Fragasso are the authors of *Your Nest Egg Game Plan* (Career Press, 2009). He is also the author of *The Thrifty Investor* (McGraw-Hill, 2000).

## About the Author

Craig is the developer of 7Twelve—a multi-asset, balanced portfolio (www.7TwelvePortfolio.com). He is also a principal at Target Date Analytics, a firm that specializes in the analysis and design of target date retirement funds (www.OnTargetIndex .com).

He is married to Tammy Trimble. They have seven children. Hobbies include running, biking, swimming, woodworking, and family vacations. He has competed in the Boston Marathon five times, but has never won.

# INDEX

## A

Accumulation phase. *See* Late
   accumulation phase
performance comparison, 91f
preretirement, 145
7Twelve portfolio, usage, 92
Accumulation portfolio.
   *See* Preretirement
   accumulation portfolio
loss, 94–95
ACME United Corporation, small-
   cap U.S. company, 11
Active 7Twelve, 133t
portfolio, active aspect, 134
Active grid, passive grid
   (contrast), 131t
Active investment,
   occurrence, 130
Actively managed fund, 129
Active mutual funds, passive
   mutual funds
   (contrast), 130
Active-passive combinations, 131
Active-passive debate,
   resolution, 135
Active portfolio management
   paradigm, 31
Active premium, consistency, 134
Aeropostale, midcap U.S.
   stock, 10
Aggregate bonds, mutual
   fund, 1, 19

Air France, non-U.S. stock, 13
Alcoa, natural resource
   company, 17
All-bond portfolio, survival rate,
   107–108
Allocation age, 93–94
chronological age, contrast,
   96–98, 98t
determination, 96–97
fixed income allocation,
   adjustment, 97
technique, usage, 114
Allocation-age portfolios, 98
All-stock portfolio
ending account balances,
   basis, 109–110
returns timing sensitivity, 110
survival rate, 108
Alternative assets, 77–78
classes, 18
America Movil, non-U.S.
   country company
   development, 13
Annually rebalanced
   portfolio
ending account value, 82, 84
ending balance, 81t
Annual rebalanced portfolio,
   growth, 82f
Annual rebalancing, 40, 59
assumption, 102
Annual returns, 57t
average, 11, 159, 162t

Annuities
  investment, 94
  purchase, 147
Artists, 7Twelve investment plan, 183t
Asset allocation model, 29–30, 89, 164–165
  asset class determination, 32–33
  formation, 96–97
Asset allocations, selection, 152–153
Asset classes, 32
  combination, 2
    7Twelve portfolio recipe, 4
  investment, 48
  performance, analysis, 32–33
  uninvestable index
    representation, 37
  variety, importance, 5
Assets
  acquisition, 147–148
  correlation, 75
  determination, 65–68
  retention, 147–148
  return patterns, 66–67
AvalonBay Communities, REIT
    fund investment, 15
Average ending balance, 83t

**B**

Balanced, term (usage), 35
Balanced funds, 138–139
  example, 149t
  list, 139t
  performance, 149–150
  risk reduction concept, 150
  usage, 138
Balanced portfolio
  asset class inclusion, 106
  example, 3f, 169f

U.S. stock/bond usage, 4
Bank of Ireland, non-U.S. stock, 13
Barclays, index maker, 41
Barclays Capital Aggregate Bond
    Index, 20
Barclays Capital U.S. Treasury
    Inflation-Protected
    Securities Index, 20
Barrick Gold Corporation,
    natural resource
    company, 17
Bond market index, 129
Bonds, 159. *See also* U.S. bonds
  age, 89
  allocation pattern, 6
  ending account balances,
    difference, 82–83
  negative returns, absence, 85–86
  portfolio, 155–156
    inclusion, reason, 19–20
  positive returns, 63
  return
    levels, 85
    strength, 165
  stocks, contrast, 19
  terminal account
    values, 85
Breadth, 24
  impact, 48–52
British Petroleum, non-U.S.
    country company
    development, 13
Broad diversification, 87
  criterion, 72
  impact, 68–73
Buy-and-hold approach, 84–85
Buy-and-hold portfolio
  ending balance, 81t
  growth, 82–83, 82f

year-end rebalancing, usage,
80, 82
Buy-and-hold rebalancing,
contrast, 80–86

# C

Capital
preservation, emphasis, 61
protection/growth, 105
Caribou Coffee Company, small-
cap U.S. company, 11
Cash, 22–23, 34
addition, impact, 71
components, annual
return, 23t
core asset class, 1, 7
ending account balances,
difference, 82–83
funds, 179t
investment, 94
negative returns, absence,
85–86
return levels, 85
terminal account values, 85
Chevron, natural resource
company, 17
Chipotle Mexican Grill, midcap
U.S. stock, 10
Chronological age, allocation
age (contrast), 96–98, 98t
Citibank, index maker, 41
Commodities
addition, 71–72
alternative asset, 77–78
correlation, 74
diversifier function, 75
funds, 178t
losses, 59–61
mutual fund, 1, 16
reference, 18
performance, 76

three-year return, 77
underwater characteristic, 76
Commodities-based mutual
fund, purchase, 17
ConocoPhillips, natural resource
company, 17
Consumer Price Index, 20
Contribution rate, 154
achievement, 156
Contributions, control,
151–152
Core 7Twelve Model, 99
Core 7Twelve portfolio, mutual
fund usage, 99
Core asset classes, 1
components, 7
Correlation
importance, 64
quantification, 73–78
Cost of living adjustment
(COLA), 106–107,
111–112
Credit Suisse, non-U.S. country
company development, 13
Critical assets, 77–78
Cumulative percentage return,
measure, 39
Cumulative return, measure, 39

# D

Default funds, usage, 138
Depth, 24
achievement, 48
impact, 48–52
Deutsche Bank, non-U.S.
country company
development, 13
Developed companies, mutual
fund, 1, 12
Developed non-U.S. stock
funds, 176t

Distribution phase, 92.
*See also* Post-retirement
distribution phase
performance comparison, 93f
retirement years, 145
Distribution portfolio, 95–96
analysis, 106–107
construction, 114, 147
losses, 111
survival, study, 111–112
Diversification
achievement, 2
avoidance, outcome, 27
benefits, 37, 59, 72
40-year analysis, 44–45
depth
representation, 48
requirement, 48–52
design, 40–46
double-edged sword, 47
forms, 5–6
impact, 26. *See also* Broad
diversification
importance, 37
increase, 69t
misunderstanding, 9
premium, 162t, 163t,
166–169
presence, 164
representation, 9
safe haven, 61
usage, 47
Diversification breadth
achievement, 50
levels, 48–49
requirement, 48–52
success, 59
Diversified portfolio, creation, 9
Diversifying assets,
categorization, 17
Diversifying funds, 7Twelve
portfolio allocation, 6

Diversity
breadth, achievement, 24
depth, achievement, 24
Dodge & Cox Balanced, 139
Dow Jones, index maker, 41
Dow Jones indexes, 126
Dow Jones Large Cap Value
Index, 118
Dow Jones Mid Cap Value, 118
Dow Jones U.S. indexes, 126
Dow Jones U.S. Large Cap Value
Index, 118
Dow Jones U.S. Mid Cap Value,
118, 121
Dow Jones U.S. Real Estate
Index, 15
Dow Jones U.S. Smallcap
Index, 11
Downside protection, 60
Downside risk, 167
Duke Realty Corporation, REIT
fund investment, 15
Dynamic asset allocation
model, 138

**E**

EAFE Index. *See* Morgan Stanley
Capital International
Europe, Asia, and Far
East Index
80/20 seven-asset portfolio,
return, 164
Electrolux, non-U.S. stock, 13
Emerging companies, mutual
fund, 1, 12
Emerging non-U.S. stocks
funds, 177t
losses, 59
Employee Benefits Research
Institute (EBRI), Issue
Brief No. 333, 153
Ending account balance, 91f, 93f

# Index

Ending account values, 51t
Ending balances, 80, 82.
    *See also* Average ending
    balance
Ending portfolio account
    balances, 84f
Ending portfolio balances
    5 percent withdrawal
        rate, 109t
    10 percent withdrawal
        rate, 110t
Engineers, 7Twelve investment
    plan, 182t
Equally weighted, seven-
    asset portfolio,
    construction, 33
Equally weighted 7Twelve
    portfolio, annual
    rebalancing, 59
Equity
    asset classes, actual risk
        (40-year period), 76t
    7Twelve portfolio
        allocation, 6
    term, usage, 4, 19
Equity allocation, 161
    80/20, 165
    100/0, 165
Equity-based mutual funds,
    inclusion, 30
Equity funds
    asset allocation, 138–139
    categorization, 17
Equity mutual fund,
        stock mutual fund
        (equivalence), 4
Equity premium, 159–163
    achievement, 167–168
    disappearance, 165
    representation, 160–161
Exchange-traded funds
    (ETFs), 129

ETF-based performance, 172
    indexes, 172
    midcap index
        representation, 10
    purchase, 17
    usage, 6, 132
    variety, 171–172
Expense ratio data, 175
ExxonMobil, large-cap U.S.
    stock, 8

## F

Fidelity Balanced fund,
    140–141
    benchmark expected return,
    142
Fidelity Freedom funds,
    140, 143
    performance, 140–141
Fidelity portfolios, 7Twelve
    portfolios (performance
    comparison), 143
Fidelity Puritan, 139
50/50 allocation, 77
Financial advisors, 7Twelve
    portfolio usage, 31–32
Five-asset portfolio,
    allocation, 71
Fixed income
    asset classes, 35
    components, terminal account
        values, 85
    performance, change
        (importance), 160–161
    term, usage, 19
Fixed income allocation
    adjustment, 97
    determination, 98
Fixed income fund, 4
    allocation, 7
    asset allocation, 138–139

40-year average annual
performance premium, 47
40-year seven-asset portfolio,
indexes (inclusion), 45t
40/60 allocation, breaking
point, 162
401(k) account
contribution rate, 152
impact, 150
401(k) retirement plan
balances, 137–138
improvement, 137
France Telecom, non-U.S.
country company
development, 13
Fund diversification, 9

**G**

General Electric (GE), large-cap
U.S. stock, 8
Geometric mean, 53
GlaxoSmithKline, non-U.S.
country company
development, 13
Glide path, 138, 139. *See also*
Target date funds
Great Wolf Resorts, small-cap
U.S. company, 11
Growth
approach, 117
premium, 122t–123t
preservation shift, 146t
relative measure, 118
U.S. equity indexes, annual
returns, 119t–120t
value, contrast, 117
Growth-oriented assets,
elimination, 124
Growth-oriented mutual fund,
usage, 117
Growth stocks, price-to-earnings
ratios, 118

**H**

High-correlation portfolio
low-correlation portfolio,
performance
comparison, 66t
risk, 67
Honda, non-U.S. country
company development,
13
Host Hotels and Resorts, REIT
fund investment, 15

**I**

Index-based 7Twelve, 172
Index funds, 8, 129
investor selection, 8–9
Individual retirement account
(IRA), contribution
rate, 152
Inflation-protected bonds,
mutual fund, 1, 19
Interasset diversification, 5–6
International bonds
funds, 179t
addition, 21–22
mutual fund, 1, 21
Intra-asset diversification, 5–6
Investable asset classes,
exposure, 4
Investment
assets, combination, 63
average annual return,
calculation, 53
categories, 32
products, diversification,
23–24
secrets, 184
Investment portfolios
change, 31
creation, 9
diversification process, 48

growth engines, 151
mechanics, 94–95
performance/return goal, 152
Investors
help, need, 153
lifecycle, 138
patience/perspective/
persistence, 156–158

**J**

Johnson & Johnson, large-cap
U.S. stock, 8

**K**

Kansas City Southern, midcap
U.S. stock, 10

**L**

Large-cap companies, mutual
fund utilization, 7
Large-cap stocks
mutual fund purchase, 10
number, 9
portfolio, 155–156
Large-cap U.S. bonds
allocation, 5
combination, 168
usage, 5
Large-cap U.S. companies,
collection, 8
Large-cap U.S. stocks, 34
allocation, 5, 49
annual return
average, 160
pattern, 74
combination, 65, 168
commodities, correlation, 66
composition, 161
discussion, 8
fund, 172, 174

example, 175t
losses, 59
negative annual returns, 73
non-U.S. stocks, correlation,
65–66
small-cap U.S. stocks
combination, 77
correlation, 74
usage, 5
value premium, 118
year-to-year performance,
73–74
Large-cap value indexes,
performance, 124–125
Large companies, mutual
fund, 1, 7
LaSalle Hotel Properties, REIT
fund investment, 15
Late accumulation phase, 90
Lehman Brothers,
disappearance, 174
Lifecycle phase, determination,
145–147
Lifecycle stage, 94
Life-stage asset allocation
models, change, 181
Life stage portfolios,
98–104
Long-run portfolio
return, 156
Losses, impact, 56–62
Low correlation, 87
diversification, increase, 69t
Low-correlation effect,
occurrence, 70–71
Low-correlation portfolio,
65–66
high-correlation portfolio,
performance comparison,
66t
Low-risk default investment
product, 138

# M

Market-cap focus, 126
Market capitalization, 8
Maximum threshold,
    representation, 39
Medium-sized companies,
    mutual fund, 1, 7
Microsoft, large-cap U.S. stock, 8
Midcap companies, mutual fund
    utilization, 7
Midcap stocks, mutual fund
    purchase, 10
Midcap U.S. equities, value
    premium, 121
Midcap U.S. stocks, 34
  examples, 10
  funds, 176t
  losses, 59
  performance, 10
Mitsubishi, non-U.S.
    country company
    development, 13
Money
  growth, 73
    measurement, reasons,
    54–56
  withdrawal, 105
Money market funds, 179t
Money market mutual funds,
    investment, 137–138
Morgan Stanley, index maker, 41
Morgan Stanley Capital
    International Europe,
    Asia, and Far East Index
    (EAFE Index), 13
Morningstar indexes, 126
Morningstar Mid Core Index, 10
Morningstar Principia data,
    usage, 9
Multi-asset 7Twelve portfolio, 4
  ending balance, 92

Multi-asset portfolio
    advantages, 73
    assembly, 114
    construction, 1
    core asset class
        representation, 34
    design, usage, 105, 113
    risk-adjusted
        performance, 150
    seven-asset portfolio,
        similarity, 106
    survival length,
        average, 111
Mutual funds (MF)
    annual returns, 57, 58t
    components, 48
    diversification
        goal, 13
    diversified investment
        product, 2
    diversity, depth
        (achievement), 24
    equal allocation, 29–30
    expense ratio, 129–130
    focus, 23–24
    negative returns, 59
    positive returns, 61
    review, 9–11
    7Twelve portfolio
        utilization, 13
    short-term performance
        basis, 152–153
    usage, 99, 129
    variety, 171–172

# N

Natural resources
    companies, examples, 17
    funds, 177t
    losses, 59
    mutual fund, 1, 16
        reference, 18

Nest egg
  guidelines, review,
      113–115
  survival, 105
Nestle, non-U.S. country
      company development,
      13
Newmont Mining, natural
      resource company, 17
99¢ Only Stores, small-cap U.S.
      company, 11
Nokia, non-U.S. country
      company development,
      13
Nominal return, 22–23
Non-U.S. bonds, 21–22, 34
  components, annual returns,
      22t
  core asset class, 7
Non-U.S. companies,
      number, 13
Non-U.S. REITs, examples, 15
Non-U.S. stocks
  addition, 70
  asset category, 34–35
  combination, 65
  components, annual returns,
      14t
  core asset class, 1, 7
  examination, 12–14
  funds, 174
      annual returns, 14
  investment advantages, 13
  underwater characteristic,
      76
  year-to-year performance,
      73–74
Norsk Hydro, non-U.S.
      stock, 13
Novartis, non-U.S.
      country company
      development, 13

**O**

One-asset portfolio
  diversification breadth,
      absence, 49
  40-year average annualized
      return, 68
  40-year period, 47t
  problem, 68
  U.S. large-cap stock
      component, 72
One-fund portfolio
  comparison, 42
  10-year average annual
      return, 43
  10-year period, 44t
100 percent bond
      portfolio, 166
100 percent stock portfolio,
      worst-case three-year
      return, 165
100/0 allocation, 186
100/0 asset allocation model,
      164–165
Outcome-based investors, 54
Overmanagement, impact, 40
Overseas Shipholding Group,
      natural resource
      company, 17

**P**

Packaging Corporation of
      America, natural resource
      company, 17
Passive 7Twelve, 133t
Passive grid, active grid
      (contrast), 131t
Passive index funds, usage, 132
Passive investment,
      occurrence, 130
Passively managed ETFs,
      usage, 134

Passively managed index-based
mutual funds, 134
Passively managed mutual
fund, 129
Passive multi-asset 7Twelve
portfolio, 31
Passive mutual funds, active
mutual funds
(contrast), 130
Pension Protection Act of 2006,
137–138
Performance
attributes, 63
examination, 121
goal, 152
measurement, 53
premium, 47
real-world measure, 55
Peugeot, non-U.S. stock, 13
Poets, 7Twelve investment
plan, 183t
Portfolio
average correlation,
decline, 71
bond inclusion, reasons,
19–20
cash, addition, 71
commodities, addition, 71–72
components, correlation
decline, 70
construction, 2–3, 61,
70, 89, 171
distribution mode, 146
diversification, 5
achievement, 169
components, variety, 6
creation, 9
downside risk, reduction, 71
effect, 67
ending account balance, 109
40-year period, risk/
performance, 46t

glide path, 138
loss
frequency, 38
recovery, math, 95t
mechanics, change, 94–96
mutual funds, inclusion, 65
partners, 77t
performance, 154
real estate, addition, 71
rebalancing, objective, 79
return. See Long-run portfolio
return
volatility, 38
risk control, 150
risk reduction, 40, 67
achievement, 102
risk-reward characteristics,
48–49
success, measure, 67
10-year annualized
return, 43
term, usage, 41
Portfolio survival
average probability, 108t
rates, impact, 107
years, number, 112t
Positive symmetry, correlation,
64
Post-retirement distribution
phase, 90
Preretirement accumulation
period, 161
portfolio, 35, 93
Preservation shift, 146t
Price-to-earnings ratio, usage,
117
Procter & Gamble, large-cap
U.S. stock, 8
Proxy performance
history, 172
Public Storage, REIT fund
investment, 15

# Index

## R

Real estate, 15–16, 34
  addition, 71
  alternative asset, 77–78
  annual returns, 16t
  core asset class, 1, 7
  diversifier function, 75
  funds, 177t
  investment, 15
  losses, 60–61
  mutual fund, 1
    investment, 15
    reference, 18
  performance, 76
  profits, 59
  three-year return, 77
Real estate investment trusts
  (REITs), 15
  mutual funds, perspective,
    15–16
Rebalancing, 24. See also Annual
  rebalancing
  benefit, 85
  buy-and-hold, contrast, 80–86
  impact, 132
  management tool, 134
  occurrence, 31
  periodic basis, 86
  premium, manifestation, 83
  schedule, selection, 86–87
  systematic intervals, 33
  systematic process, 79
  time frame, 79–80
Resources, 16–19
  components, annual
    returns, 18t
  core asset class, 1, 7
  mutual funds, separation,
    16–17
Retirement accounts
  contribution, 153

investment, 105
Retirement nest egg, survival
  probability, 114
Retirement portfolio
  asset classes representation, 106
  construction/usage,
    components, 113
  money, withdrawal, 105
  performance expectations,
    irrationality, 153
  return, generation, 154
Retirement year, 144t–145t
  examples. See Target
    retirement year
  target date representation, 146
Return
  chasing, problem, 152–156
  goal, 152
  portfolios, 137
  standard deviation, increase,
    11, 39
  timing, all-stock portfolio
    sensitivity, 110
Risk, 159
  definitions, 39–40
  frequency measurement, 51
  loss magnitude
    measurement, 50
  measurement, 38–40
  reduction, 44, 137. See also
    Portfolio
    improvement, 50
  tolerance, 90
Risk-adjusted performance, 2,
  33, 56, 150
Risk-based implementation
  plan, 98
Risk measures, 49
  standard deviation, usage, 75
  three-year cumulative percent
    return, usage, 75
  usefulness, 42

Risk-return trade-off, 163
Rolling annualized returns,
 155f, 157f
Rolling period, shortening, 157
Ross Stores, midcap U.S.
 stock, 10
Roth IRA account balance,
 position, 97
Royal Caribbean Cruises, non-
 U.S. stock, 13
Rules-based portfolio,
 performance, 34
Russell, index maker, 41
Russell 2000 Index, 11
Russell indexes, 126
Russell Midcap Index, 10

**S**

Samsung Electronics, non-
 U.S. country company
 development, 13
Saving years, 91–94
Sealed Air Corporation, natural
 resource company, 17
Seven-asset portfolio
 diversification premium, 164
 evolution, 34–35
 examination, 68
 40-year average annual
  return, 46
 40-year correlation, 74t
 40-year period, 47t
 historical performance,
  basis, 45
 multi-asset portfolio, s
  imilarity, 106
 100/0 allocation, 166
 performance basis, 73
 rebalancing example, 80
 research, principles, 34
 return, increase, 163, 165

7Twelve portfolio subset, 38
two-asset portfolio,
 contrast, 161
 usage, 44
7Twelve design, 30
7Twelve investment plan, 182t,
 183t
7Twelve Life Stage 50-60, 99
 ending account value, 142
 portfolio, allocation
  assignation, 99, 101
7Twelve Life Stage 60-70, 99
 ending account value, 142
 portfolio allocation
  assignation, 101
7Twelve Life Stage 70+, 99
 model, allocation
  assignation, 101
 portfolio, return, 141
7Twelve Life Stage models,
 consideration, 101
7Twelve Life Stage portfolios,
 100t
 annual returns, 102, 103t
7Twelve perfection, secrets/
 principles, 181
7Twelve plan, usage, 182t
7Twelve portfolio
 allocation, 6
 annualized return, 26
 annual rebalancing, 93
 annual returns, 25t, 58t
 approach, 139–145
 asset allocation, 31
 components
  40-year performance
   history, absence, 38
  performance history,
   absence, 73
  rebalancing, 24, 26
 construction, actively manged
  funds (usage), 132

debut, 35
diversification, 37, 61
  breadth, achievement, 50
  premium, 168t
equity-based mutual funds,
  inclusion, 30
equity funds, 126
equity portion,
  representation, 92
ETFs
  performance data, usage,
    173t
  raw indexes, usage, 174t
example, 3f, 169f
financial advisor usage, 31–32
fixed income asset classes, 35
function, 133
holdings
  number, 24t
  redundancy, 23–24
list, 139t
losses, 60
monthly growth, 56f
mutual funds
  diversification, 3
  raw indexes, usage, 174t
one-fund portfolio,
  comparison, 50
percent annual returns,
  rebalancing schedules
  (usage), 86t
performance, 24, 26, 171
principles, 184
recipe, 1–4, 30
representation, 2
returns, generation, 167
salsa, metaphor, 4–7
tax efficiency, 80
10-year growth, 54t
10-year period, 44t
two-fund portfolio,
  comparison, 50

value/growth allocations, 126t
7Twelve value bias, 125–127
Simon Property Group, REIT
  fund investment, 15
Single-asset portfolio, final
  balance, 92
65 percent equity/35 percent
  fixed income asset
  allocation model, 30
60/40 allocation level, 167
60/40 asset allocation model,
  performance, 139
60/40 balanced fund,
  allocation, 5
60/40 balanced mix, 155
60/40 balanced model, 6
60/40 balanced return, 141–142
60/40 portfolio, 63, 156, 163
  ending balance, 93
  monthly growth, 56f
60/40 stocks/bonds, ten-year
  growth, 54t
Small-cap companies, mutual
  fund utilization, 7
Small-cap growth, ending
  balance, 121
Small-cap U.S. companies,
  examples, 11
Small-cap U.S. stocks, 34
  combination, 65
  large-cap U.S. stocks
    combination, 77
    correlation, 74
  losses, 59
  year-to-year performance,
    73–74
Small-cap value funds, 176t
Small companies, mutual
  fund, 1, 7
Southern Union Company,
  natural resource
  company, 17

Southwest Airlines, stock
   purchase, 19
Spending years, 91–94
Standard deviation,
   usefulness, 42
Standard & Poor's, index
   maker, 41
Standard & Poor's 500 Index
   funds, 8
   investor selection, 8–9
   profits, 60
   usage, 9
   returns, 160
Standard & Poor's 500 Index
   (S&P500), 8
Standard & Poor's Goldman
   Sachs Commodity
   Index, 17
Standard & Poor's
   indexes, 126
Standard & Poor's Midcap 400
   Index, 10
Standard & Poor's Smallcap 600
   Index, 11
Stock market index, 129
Stock mutual fund, equity
   mutual fund
   (equivalence), 4
Stocks, 159. *See also*
   U.S. stocks
   allocation pattern, 6
   bonds, contrast, 19
   funds, negative returns, 26
   performance,
      potential/risk, 63
   term, usage, 4
Strategic management, 87
Strategic portfolio
   guidelines, 29
   passive approach, 29
Strategic portfolio design, 29
Survival, term (usage), 107

**T**

T. Rowe Price Asset Allocation
   Glide-Path Strategy,
   153–154
T. Rowe Price Balanced, 139
Tactical management, 87
Target date,
   representation, 138
Target date funds
   assumption, problem, 148
   design, 142, 148
   glide path, risk reduction
      concept, 150
   inappropriateness, 146
   introduction, 138–139
   list, 139t
   mismatch, 147–150
   performance, 140, 148–149
   perspective, 146–147
   usage, 138, 168
Target funds, example, 149t
Target retirement year,
   examples, 140t, 143t
Telecom Corporation of
   New Zealand, non-U.S.
   stock, 13
10-year analysis, 7Twelve
   portfolio
   (usage), 41t
10-year portfolio, risk/
   performance, 42t
Terminal account values, 85
Time frames
   examination, 159–166
   example, 160t
Timing risk, increase, 114
TIPS. *See* Treasury Inflation
   Protected Bonds
Total portfolio transition, 102
Toyota, non-U.S. country
   company development, 13

Transition phase, retirement
  preparation, 145
Treasury Inflation Protected
  Bonds (TIPS), 20, 59, 99
  basis, 101
  funds, 179t
  investment, 94 ·
Twelve-fund portfolio, two-fund
  portfolio (contrast), 3f
20/80 asset allocation,
  superiority, 162
Two-asset 60/40 portfolio,
  annualized return, 72
Two-asset portfolio
  diversification breadth,
    absence, 49
  diversification premium,
    absence, 164
  ending balance, 92
  40-year period, 47t
  40-year return, 70
  low-correlation portfolio
    criterion, 72
  return, 165
  risk reduction, improvement,
    50
  risk-reward characteristics,
    49–50
  seven-asset portfolio, contrast,
    161
  10-year return, 167
  three-year cumulative percent
    loss, 70
Two-fund 60/40 portfolio,
  improvement, 51
Two-fund 60 percent stock/40
  percent bond portfolio,
  rebalancing, 55
Two-fund portfolio
  annual returns, 102
  comparison, 43
  depiction, 55

10-year period, 44t
twelve-fund portfolio,
  contrast, 3f

**U**

Underlying mutual funds, 1
Undersaving, problem, 151
U.S. bonds, 19–21, 34
  components, annual
    returns, 21t
  core asset class, 1
  funds, 178t
  historical performance, 160
  investment, achievement, 20
U.S. cash, mutual fund, 1, 22
U.S. global fixed income
  diversification,
    achievement, 21
U.S. intermediate government
  bonds, 159
U.S. large-cap stock
  investment (S&P500 Index),
    74
  portfolio, cumulative loss, 42
U.S. large stocks, monthly
  growth, 56f
U.S. stocks
  asset class, total allocation, 7
  components, annual
    returns, 12t
  core asset class, 1, 7
  examination, 7–12
  market, negative returns, 55
  10-year growth, 54f
U.S. Treasury bills, nominal
  return, 22–23

**V**

Value
  annual returns, 119t–120t

Value (*Continued*)
 approach, 117
 bias. *See* 7Twelve value bias
 growth, contrast, 117
 premium, 118, 122t–123t
  frequency, 125t
 relative measure, 118
 term, usage, 117
Value funds, investment,
  137–138
Value-oriented mutual funds,
  selection, 125
Value stock,
  classification, 117
Value tilt
 long-run advantage, 124
 reward, 125–126
Vanguard Wellington, 139
Volatility, measurement,
  38–40

**W**

Wealth, accumulation, 90–91
Weyerhauser, natural resource
  company, 17
Withdrawal rate, 111, 113
 assumption, 108
Worst-case performance,
  measure, 39
Worst-case return, 38

**Y**

Your age in bonds, 89, 98

**Z**

0/100 allocation
 20/80 allocation,
  comparison, 162
 downside protection, 167